getting over it
God's way

rebuilding the ruins of your wounded heart

Edye Burrell

WESTBOW
PRESS
A DIVISION OF THOMAS NELSON

WestBow Press
A Division of Thomas Nelson
1663 Liberty Drive
Bloomington, IN 47403
www.westbowpress.com
1-(866) 928-1240

ISBN: 978-1-4497-0444-5 (sc)
ISBN: 978-1-4497-0445-2 (dj)
ISBN: 978-1-4497-0483-4 (e)

Library of Congress Control Number: 2010935748

Interior and cover design by Ashley Brooke Burrell Beasley
Cover photograph by Shutterstock

WestBow Press rev. date: 9/24/2010

Printed in the United States of America

Acknowledgements

There would be no book if not for my Lord and Savior, Jesus Christ, who chose me to be His own and placed within me His Holy Spirit to patiently and tenderly teach me these truths and transform my life through them.

I am deeply grateful to my husband, Lee, whose love for me and passion for Jesus Christ, encourages me to pursue wholeheartedly the things God has called me to do. He is my most faithful supporter and the one who models to me the way our Lord calls us to live out our faith in Him.

My precious, creative daughter, Brooke, has worked countless hours to edit, format, and design this book. God has gifted her with remarkable creativity and with a heart for Him. She is able to capture not only my heart, but the heart of God, and the result is a masterpiece that is able to capture the heart of the reader, as well.

I am also thankful for two amazing friends: Cindy Jones, my soul mate and partner in the shared vision of the ministry this writing will launch, and Melody Taylor, a tender, teachable soul whose enthusiasm for God spurs me on. Both of these women have encouraged me throughout this process by reading, critiquing, praying, and pushing me forward when I wanted to give up. They have applied these truths to their own wounds and have become witnesses with me to their transforming power.

Contents

Chapter 1

∾

Am I the Only One?

Why is everyone else so happy?
Am I the only one living in pain?
What did I do to deserve this?
Can't anyone see how badly I'm hurting?
Who can I talk to that will understand?

My heart aches for those of you who are living in the pain of your wounds. I have lived with the loneliness of a hurting heart and for many years allowed it to dominate my life. But I'd like to offer you some comfort—there is relief and healing. And I hope you will allow me to accompany you on your journey.

Nothing makes us feel more isolated and alone than the pain of a wounded heart. While we may know in our heads that we are not the only ones dealing with painful circumstances, our hearts tell us that we are utterly alone, that no one could possibly understand our pain. And if anyone did know, would they really care?

At some point we find ourselves asking, "Am I the only one who hurts?"

If that question has ever crossed your mind, let me assure you that you are not alone. The people you rub shoulders with every day are dealing with pain at some level. Their hearts have been wounded in some way. The lives of people all around you have been, or will be, turned upside down at some point.

If we felt the freedom to share our pain, if we knew that talking about it with another person would bring compassion and tenderness, we would open our hearts to others and see that we're not alone. We would be able to stand with one another and help each other move toward healing and wholeness.

But the reality for those with wounded hearts seems to be that most of us have tried to open up at times but were greeted with dismissal, judgment or indifference. Since we did not received the compassion, tenderness, or grace we needed to move toward healing, our pain and loneliness deepened. We learn to hide our pain, or at least the real reason for it, and put on a mask proclaiming to the world that we're okay. Everything is under control. We get up each day and put on a confident, happy mask that declares, "I'm tough. I can handle whatever life throws my way." Our mask may even tell others that we hurt, but only because we are the victims of life's unfairness.

Whatever facade we put up isolates us from others. It keeps us from having meaningful, intimate relationships, and it holds us in pain and isolation.

What we don't understand in our feeling of aloneness is that we are surrounded by other wounded people who feel the same way; people who, like us, are seeking someone to open up to, someone to share their hearts with. *We fail to see that wounded people who cannot deal with their own pain and brokenness are incapable of helping us deal with ours.*

Knowing this won't lessen the pain of your wounded heart, but I hope it will help you feel less isolated. My prayer is that you will be encouraged to drop the facade and open the door for at least one person to walk with you on your journey out of woundedness.

If you will do that, you will quickly find this world we live in is full of wounded people. Why? What is it about human beings that cause us to hurt and be hurt throughout our lives?

God answers that question for us in Isaiah 53:6, "We all, like sheep, have gone astray, each of us has turned to his own way...." Romans 3:23 declares, "For all have sinned and fall short of the glory of God."

We are hurt and we hurt others because this world is full of what God calls "sin." When you hear the word *sin* you might think of people who have done horrible and evil things, but God defines sin as nothing more than each of us going our own way, instead of His way.

The sin that has wounded many of us, however, typically comes from someone's selfish disregard for the feelings of others, rather than an evil act. The sin that wounds our hearts isn't always an action against us such as physical abuse, words that tear us down, or the taking of something dear. Our hearts can also be wounded by the sin of inaction. This occurs when someone withholds something from us—love, boundaries, affirmation, discipline, or time—that is necessary to our becoming the person God created us to be. When this happens it's easy for us to see someone else's inaction as sin. On the other hand, when we are the ones withholding or neglecting, we are quick to dismiss our own sinful behavior by justifying it as a necessary way to deal with a situation. We tell ourselves that the person was not deserving of our love, affirmation, or time.

We don't mind labeling these things as sin when someone else does them, but when it comes to our actions, we'd rather call them something else. Sometimes we know we are wrong even as we make our excuses, but other times we honestly don't see the wrongness of our actions. We make ourselves feel better by believing that others would have said or done the same thing had they been in the same situation.

When sin entered the world, at the time of Adam and Eve, something else entered alongside it—pain. Sin brought with it the pain of rejection, lies, loss, pride, selfishness, and evil of every kind. This pain gave sin wounding power.

Sin wounds us every time it touches us, and it brings nothing but pain. Though it can feel pleasant momentarily, we shouldn't be deceived into believing that the brief satisfaction we feel somehow makes sin okay. Sin wounds both the one being targeted, and also the one engaging in the sin.

Scripture tells us in Romans 5:12 that "sin entered the world through one man [Adam], and death through sin, and in this way death came to all men, because all sinned." We are all born with a sin nature, which separates us from God. Because God created us in His image and designed us to live in an intimate relationship with Him—not just to believe in Him but to know Him through a vital, growing relationship—separation from God wounds us.

When Jesus died on the cross and rose again, He made a personal relationship with God possible. When we are separated from God, we miss the very essence of who we are meant to be.

Sin and separation from God create a void in our hearts that only He can fill. Though we go through life trying to fill the void with any manner of things and people, nothing but God will ever fill the void in a way that satisfies our deepest longings and needs.

If separation from God was the only wound of sin, that would be quite enough, but sin brings other wounds into our lives. As sinful creatures, we wound others and others wound us every day. There's not a person who has not inflicted pain by their own hurtful words and deeds or suffered pain from someone else's. Though some of us have been more deeply wounded than others, we all carry the evidence of sin's destructive wounds.

Picture your heart as a brick wall that is damaged every time the effects of sin touch it. Some sins touch us in small ways, just chipping out a piece of mortar: the criticism of a boss who discourages you, or the snippiness of a friend that hurts your feelings, the insensitivity of a co-worker, or embarrassing, inappropriate humor directed your way. Many times the touch of sin comes from someone close.

Often we damage our own hearts by demeaning ourselves. How many of us have made a mistake, slapped ourselves on the forehead and called ourselves "stupid"? I do things like that to myself on a regular basis, becoming my own worst enemy, and every time I do, the enemy whispers in my ear, "You're right." If we do that enough, we start believing our own destructive remarks, don't we?

Whether the sins come to us or from us, our response is often the same—we brush them off as if they were nothing, but they aren't. They open the door for another "small" something to chip out yet another piece of mortar in the wall of our hearts. You see, once we are wounded even in a small way, our hearts are on the alert, waiting to be hurt again because we are now more vulnerable to pain. I can't tell you how many times my already hurting heart has been crushed by an innocent remark or action that hit me right where I was the most vulnerable.

When we don't deal with these small wounds, they eventually become big and before long enough mortar has been chipped away, causing a brick in the wall of our hearts to fall to the ground. Losing just one brick puts every other part of our heart's wall in the precarious position of waiting to be damaged, if not destroyed.

Small hurts plant seeds in our minds that Satan uses to grow thriving lies masked as insecurity, poor self-image, lack of self-confidence, worthlessness, fear of failure, or feelings of inadequacies, suspicion, jealousy, and even pride.

We have all had those days when something seemingly insignificant happens, like the rudeness of the checkout girl at the grocery store. We blow it off, not realizing that her behavior left a scratch on the wall of our hearts. Add to her rudeness someone cutting us off in traffic on the way home and our angry outburst toward the other driver, and now we have "our tail in a major twist." The scratch becomes a cut. By the time the kids come home grumpy, our little scratch from the rude checkout girl has turned into a festering sore that makes us feel as though the whole world is out to get us. After mother calls to complain because we haven't called her, we are propelled into morbid self-examinations to figure out what is wrong with us that made the whole world turn against us or what is wrong with everyone else that leaves us thinking we are the only normal people on the planet. Either way we have had a no good, very bad day instead of a day filled with joy and fulfillment, all because a check-out girl chose to take her bad day out on us.

Maybe you've had the proverbial bad hair day. Most women have! Instead of taking what your hair gives you and going about your business, you pitch a mini-fit for the enemy to capitalize on. By the time your fit comes to an end, Satan has convinced you that you have the worst head of hair in the world—and you're also ugly! In your perceived ugliness you decide that you're not only ugly but unlovely and unloved. You tell yourself that since no one loves you, you might as well add a fat body to your bad hair, so you go to the pantry and dive in to some Chips Ahoy. With every bite, you feel uglier, more unlovely, and more unloved. You begin to feel guilt and shame and see yourself as a total failure with no self-control. What started as a little trouble getting your hair to cooperate has turned into a full-fledged war against your self-worth. By the end of the day, you are telling yourself that you should just eat cold worms and die, because the world would be better off without you.

These two scenarios may sound ridiculous, but most of us have lived through at least one of them, probably both.

Do you see how one sinful thought or action, coming from yourself or another person, can start out as only a scratch but then fester into a gaping wound in your heart? Do you see how one piece of mortar chipped out of the wall of your heart can send you into a downward spiral that creates a hole with the potential to cause the entire wall to come tumbling down, leaving your heart a broken mess?

Sometimes sin comes at us like a wrecking ball tearing our heart apart in one fell swoop. The sudden death of a loved one, the betrayal of a friend, the cruelty of a parent, the loss of something precious, the death of a dream, a choice gone dreadfully wrong, or hope turned to devastation—all of these can suddenly break our hearts, killing the very essence of who God created us to be. The wounds left by the effect of this magnitude of sin can rob us of our innocence, our joy, and, worst of all, our hope for having a "normal" life.

The evidence of our wounds manifests itself in the way we view ourselves, the way we treat others, behaviors that attract attention whether good or bad, the way we view our world, and most significantly the way we view God.

In an effort to cope with our pain we construct a grid for survival through which we view every aspect of our lives. Our grid may serve to protect us from more pain or keep others at arm's length. Many live their entire lives hiding behind a facade so no one can see who they really are. Others perfect the art of listening, asking questions, and showing interest in others for the purpose of drawing them in while never revealing anything significant about themselves or their lives. Too many people live their entire lives never allowing anyone to get too close, all because they believe that being known or loved means being hurt.

Our personal grid may help us to feel significant, influential, or powerful. I'm sure you know people who are driven to perfection, people who can never have enough money or things, women who are obsessed with their physical appearance, men who lift weights until they look like the Incredible Hulk, or someone who is constantly tooting his or her own horn. From the outside looking in, these people seem to have a wonderful life, to have it all together. We can't see the hidden pain that drives their behavior—the pain of insecurity or worthlessness pushing them to constantly prove their adequacy.

Our grid may fill a need we have to be in control of our environment, our circumstances, or the people in our lives. I operated from this grid for many years. I grew up feeling totally out of control of most of the things that concerned me. I believed the only thing under my control was the condition of my bedroom, so I made sure I kept it immaculate. My space didn't include disorder or dust bunnies. Much of my spare time was spent bringing more order and cleanliness to an already organized, almost sterile room. This compulsion for order and cleanliness followed me to college and then into marriage and motherhood. I believed that if my physical environment was out of order, so was the rest of my life.

Because my survival grid was control, I can now spot a control freak from a mile away. I recognize those who are so compulsive about their physical environment, their time, and their own agenda that they are willing to sacrifice the people around them on the altar of perfect order.

Most of us have observed people who exert their power and control over others through intimidation, cruelty, criticism, or threats.

Others distort caring and kindness into a means of controlling the people in their lives. They always seem to be kind and loving, to have others' best interest at heart, and to say the right words at just the right time. The operative word here is "always." When a person is "always" these things, I get very nervous. Only one person is always these things: Jesus.

We should be careful of those who "always" do and say the right thing, because we may be dealing with someone who has a steel grip on their emotions, someone afraid to let their guard down for fear of an eruption of the emotions simmering just below the surface.

Have you ever watched a person finagle every situation so that he or she is the one who comes out on top? Do you scratch your head wondering how they manage to make even the worst case scenario work to their advantage? These people operate through the grid of controlling every circumstance in their lives.

We all must identify our grid and the purpose it serves because the longer we live with the pain of our wounds, whether big or small, the more that grid becomes embedded in our minds and hearts. You may believe that your grid is necessary for your life and your sanity because it makes you feel safe, protected, and in control. Though you may not see it, your survival grid is motivated by fear, and that fear has become so deeply ingrained that it is sucking the very life out of you.

Reflection & Application

1. In what ways has the pain of your wounds made you feel isolated and alone?

2. Can you identify places in your life where you feel the void your pain has created? How have you tried to fill that void?

3. Describe the survival grid that you have put in place.

Chapter 2

☙

God, Is My Pain Your Plan?

The words, actions, and attitudes that wound our hearts come at us from myriad sources. Sometimes we see the hurt coming because we know the one wounding us and have grown to expect it. Though expecting it doesn't lessen the pain, it allows us to brace ourselves for the inevitable blow.

Other times the pain takes us completely by surprise, leaving us no time to prepare for the wound we are about to receive. These wounds throw us off balance and cause us to move into a hyper-vigilant state, always watching and wondering if the pain will come again and from where.

Some of us have been wounded by significant people in our lives—those who are supposed to love us or care for us, those whose authority we have been taught to honor and obey, those who have pledged friendship or companionship, or those who have entered into a covenant relationship with us.

These are the worst kind of wound because they come to us through no fault of our own. We are most often the *unsuspecting* victim the first time we are wounded, and then the *unwilling* victim for as long as the pain is inflicted. *The wounds caused by these significant people can shape our lives; they often damage the depths of our souls and rob us of our innocence.*

These wounds are especially devastating because they break our trust and distort the way we view every other relationship in our lives, including our relationship with God. The wounds caused by significant people keep some from placing their trust in God because they believe He has somehow inflicted their pain. This same deceptive mindset can keep believers from ever seeking an intimate relationship with God.

When wounds are caused by those we should be able to trust we feel totally alone. We don't know where to turn, because the one who should comfort us in our pain is the source of our pain.

This is the kind of pain that prompted David to cry out in Psalm 55:12-14a, "If an enemy were insulting me, I could endure it; if a foe were raising himself against me, I could hide from him. But it is you, a man like myself, my companion, my close friend, with whom I once enjoyed sweet fellowship."

Have you felt this kind of pain? If you have, you know that nothing hurts worse than the pain inflicted by one whose love and care we have trusted. Like so many others, I am intimately acquainted with the wounds caused by significant people in my life. I grew up with an angry, controlling dad who beat the living day lights out of us under the guise of giving a spanking. My father didn't want us to cry during these "spankings" because he couldn't stand the sound of our crying. In an effort to pacify him we held our breath to keep from crying. Then came the sound … you know, the pathetic sound of a sob breaking loose while you are trying desperately to hold your breath. That sound sent my father into a rage every time, and we would get "spanked" again. I learned early not to cry outwardly, but I was crying on the inside. My tears stopped at a young age and I didn't cry again, except in anger, until God began to heal me many years later. My father had expectations that no child could satisfy. I never felt loved, accepted, or worthwhile, but I did feel rejected, inadequate, and worthless. I felt the painful abuse of the father who was supposed to love me, care for me, and protect me.

Worse than the physical abuse was the deception we engaged in when other people were around. No matter what had been going on, when the doorbell rang, we became the perfect family. That deception caused me to imagine that my home was normal. I was convinced that my friends' parents were nice when I was there and like my parents when no one else was around. There was no way of knowing any differently because I didn't talk about the secrets of my home, and I believed that my friends were keeping quiet about their secrets, too.

There are countless others who are intimately acquainted with the broken trust and betrayal of significant people in their lives. Their stories could be told from now 'til the end of time, and we would never tell them all. So I will share just a few to help ease the burden of your pain as you see that you are not the only one who hurts.

The young woman had saved herself for marriage. She was thrilled when she met the young man in the singles group at church. She had no idea on her wedding day that the man she was giving her heart to would shatter it into a million pieces. She didn't know that this Christian man she was entrusting her future to was addicted to pornography. For eight years the secret was kept from her as the anger and guilt her husband felt toward himself was projected outward in her direction. She didn't know what was going on, only that this marriage she had dreamed of all her life was bringing her deep pain. She had no idea, either, that the pain she felt would be multiplied a hundred fold when her husband's secret life was exposed. Her trusted friend had betrayed her beyond belief, and she despaired almost to death. The only thing that kept her alive was the child she carried, the child of her betrayer. Would there ever be joy in her life again? Did anyone understand the pain she was feeling? Where was God and why had He let this happen?

In our deepest pain we all ask these kinds of questions.

The little boy asked these questions in his child-like way the day his father walked out on his family. Through his sobs of pain, fear, and uncertainty the little boy screamed in anger, "I don't want to be in this family anymore." Instead of being comforted in the arms of one who loved him, he was put out on the front porch on that cold winter night with his suitcase and told to find another home. Eventually he was let back into the house, but can you imagine the terrible wound that was left in this little boy's heart? His father was gone, and it seemed that those left behind could not be trusted to comfort and care for him either.

We human beings have an uncanny ability to deeply hurt those we love the most. Our selfishness causes us to say and do things that we may regret later; then, often our pride kicks in and prevents us from righting the wrong. Leaving wrongs unresolved allows them to do their most damaging work. This is a greater act of selfishness than the wounding itself, for it leaves the wounds to grow deep enough to destroy lives.

I don't understand why it is so hard for us to say the words, "I'm sorry" or "I was wrong. Will you please forgive me?" These are such healing words. They are a soothing balm to the heart that has been wounded. Yet these words of life are often withheld because we are too prideful or embarrassed to admit our sin and say them. If you struggle with using these words in abundance, I pray that you will learn to say them often and with great sincerity. We all wound others simply because we are sinful creatures, and we have daily opportunities to practice using these precious life-giving words.

Some of us have betrayed ourselves and are living with self-inflicted wounds. Many have bought into Satan's lie that we can somehow escape the consequences of our own prideful, naïve, or just plain stupid choices. As a result we live with the aftermath of those choices.

She was such a daydreamer, always getting sidetracked and forgetting to do what she was told. When she went to school, her teachers had to call her back from "the zone" throughout the day. She felt so stupid. While her classmates were learning, she was struggling just to pay attention. It took a few years, but finally she was tested and diagnosed with A.D.D. Her family and teachers worked hard to help her rise above the A.D.D.

The disorder had wounded her by making her feel different and dumb, but she was determined to be an overcomer until she realized that she could use her "condition" as an excuse. That is when her self-inflicted wounds began. Throughout her teens and early adulthood she used the A.D.D. as her excuse to get out of doing things she didn't enjoy or felt were hard. It became her excuse in marriage to leave the house unkempt, the meals unprepared, the laundry undone, and the bills unpaid. She was wounding herself, her husband, her children, and her marriage.

She was wasting her talents and creativity, living way below her potential. But what was she to do? She had chosen to live as a "disabled" person for so long that she had convinced herself she couldn't live any other way. She believed she had lost her chance to be an overcomer.

The pain of self-inflicted wounds is no less damaging than the wounds caused by others. Our self-inflicted wounds still hurt very deeply and take us to the same destructive places as any other kind of wound.

He was born with cerebral palsy. With it came challenges that caused both physical and emotional wounds. As a young boy, he dreamed of playing sports and being part of a team. He loved football and always wanted to play, but for him it was not an option because only one side of his body works properly. As a child, he was wounded every day as he was seen as the "different one." He was wounded by those who did not include him and treated him differently.

When he reached his teens, instead of listening to the voices of those who loved and valued him, this young man chose to believe what the other kids had told him, "You are different." He told himself that he didn't care what other people thought, but he did. He began to withdraw from everyday life, skipping school on a daily basis for weeks at a time. Although he was a straight-A student, he chose to focus on what he was missing rather than what he had, and in doing so added self-inflicted wounds to the wounds inflicted by his physical limitations and those who treated him differently because of them.

She was smart, pretty, reared in a Christian home, and gave her life to Christ when she was in second grade. She was well-liked and respected by her peers. Even though academics were very important to her, there was a problem—she felt that what people saw when they looked at her was "a big brain with two legs sticking out." She wanted to be popular for more than her intelligence. She found her chance to begin again as someone other than "the really smart girl" when she went to college 800 miles from home. There she began to search for her significance apart from God, who had always before defined her worth.

Her search led her to drugs that "expanded her mind." She found herself doing all the things she said she would never do: drugs, sex, and allowing herself to be in abusive relationships. Eventually she gave up her dream to go to law school and the future she had planned for herself in order to be a single mom to her son.

Those of us with self-inflicted wounds often believe we don't deserve anything better than the pain we are living with. This is why we tend to make the same poor choices over and over again.

Those who have brought pain on themselves often lose faith in their ability to make good choices or to accurately assess people or situations.

Recently I taught the "Getting Over It God's Way" seminar, and sitting in the audience was a woman who was on her third marriage, all three to alcoholic husbands. We shake our heads in disbelief, but this cycle is more common than we think. It's not just bad marriages; it is all kinds of poor, destructive choices that cause us to revisit the same place time and again while we are hoping with all of our hearts that surely our next choice will take us somewhere different.

Because we imagine that others are judging us, we often believe we have nowhere to turn. We feel that no one really cares that we're hurting.

Sometimes this is true. There can be two conflicting responses to the consequences we suffer as a result of our own sinful choices. Our world tells us that it is our life and we have every right to live it the way we want to—that it is nobody's business but our own and that everything will be alright. The church often tells us that we are getting what we deserve and that we shouldn't expect sympathy for the consequences we are suffering. After all, we made our bed and now we have to lie in it. Both of these responses only deepen the pain of our wounds because one releases us from personal responsibility and the other sends us down the path of shame and guilt.

Others are wounded by sin that touches them from afar, wounds perpetrated on them by the fallen world we live in, where cruelty, death, and disease inevitably touch our lives.

The symptoms came on suddenly: the headaches, nausea, and extremely high blood pressure. He was admitted to the hospital for tests to determine why his blood pressure was off the charts at the age of twenty. He never imagined that he would hear, "Your kidneys have shut down." Why? How could that possibly be? When would they start working again? Within a week his doctor delivered the unwelcome news that would change his life, "Your kidneys aren't coming back." In that moment everything changed.

His college education was interrupted in the middle of the semester and he had a choice to make: dialysis, which would interrupt his life for four hours a day, three times a week and wreak havoc on his body, or a transplant, which meant for the rest of his life taking immune-suppressing drugs with all their side effects. This may not sound like a wound, but it was an event that came out of nowhere to turn this young man's life upside down. His life would never be the same because of a disease that entered the world long ago along with sin.

When God created man, sin and the wounds it causes were not in His plan. He had planned for us a perfect world void of death, pain, disease, and anything else that would corrupt an intimate love relationship with Him. We know that world as the Garden of Eden.

Because God did not want a relationship with robots, He gave us free will to choose to live His way or our own. Sadly, man and woman chose their own way, and here we are with sin touching us every day, robbing us of the life God intended for us.

She heard it on the news. Two women in her apartment complex had been raped by a well-groomed man in a business suit. The rapist was still at large. The rapes had happened in the parking lot she had to walk through each night when she got home from work. Would she be next? This woman was afraid, and with each passing day that the rapist was still out there, her fear grew. Several months passed with no more attacks, but that did nothing to put her mind at ease. She saw a rapist around every corner. She was constantly looking over her shoulder at home, at work, at the mall, in the Laundromat, and in every parking lot, not just her own. She tried to get her fear under control, but it was overwhelming her. She suspected every man in a business suit, including the men at her office. Then she began to wonder if the rapist had changed his look. This sin had touched her through the news on TV, but it had wounded her with a deep, irrational, constant fear that was affecting her work, her relationships, and her mental well-being.

The reality is that it doesn't matter who or what the perpetrator of your wound is—a significant person in your life, yourself, or the fallen world you live in—they still hurt and the pain they cause destroys a part of your heart. It destroys you because you were never meant to be wounded by sin, death, or disease, or to experience the pain they bring to your life.

Reflection & Application

1. Who or what has wounded your heart?

2. How has your response to your own pain caused you to hurt those you
    love and care for, or even further hurt yourself?

3. Are you living with the painful consequences of your own choices?
    Take some time to journal about the destructive places your self-
    inflicted wounds have taken you.

Chapter 3

∾

I'm Just FINE, Thank Ya Ma'am

When God created Adam and Eve, He placed them in the Garden of Eden. It was a perfect world where all their needs were met by their Creator. If they had not eaten the fruit from the Tree of Knowledge, or if Adam had been man enough to say no to Eve, we would all still be in the Garden. You see, God didn't intend for us to have the knowledge of evil. Everything He desires for us is good!

Because we were created to live in a world without sin, pain, sickness, and death, we are not equipped to deal with our heart wounds by ourselves, but that hasn't stopped us from trying. While we should be trying to find healing for our wounds, we instead try to ignore them, overcome them, or somehow rise above them. And worse, we try to do it alone.

Our deepest desire is for others to know our pain, share it with us, comfort us, and give us hope that the pain will go away. But what would people think if they knew how badly we are hurting and how inadequate we are to stop the pain ourselves? Would they see us as wimpy and weak? Or worse, would others believe we are responsible for whatever wounded us? Fearing what others will think causes us to hide our pain. *Our pain creates in us a feeling of aloneness that Satan uses to isolate us.*

As deeply as we desire for others to know and care, we often have such a great fear of exposure that we would rather remain alone. In our isolation Satan tells us that no one will ever understand the pain in our hearts, and even if someone did, they wouldn't care. The enemy wants us to remain fearful, wounded and in pain, because as long as we are, we're not really living at all, we merely exist. As long as we merely exist, we can't reflect the love and grace of God to the world.

When we are wounded, even just a little, and we don't deal with it quickly and properly, our wounds begin to fester and our pain intensifies. At some point the pain exceeds our pain-tolerance level, and we begin to act out in our pain. We have outburst of anger or bouts of self-pity. We wall off our hearts and develop a hard exterior or we struggle with the emotions of depression. We become consumed with fear and suspicion or we disengage from our emotions so that we don't have to feel.

When our pain is exposed we are often confronted with conflicting counsel. There are those who are waiting to jump on our bandwagon and help us make excuses for our behavior, people who tell us that we have every right to be angry or discouraged or feel like a "nobody" or be fearful after what was done to us. They even encourage us to make the offender pay for causing us pain.

There are others who pat us on the back and "bless our hearts" telling us that we are "poor little things." They assure us that we are indeed victims. Still others want to negate our feelings by telling us, "Oh, no, you shouldn't feel that way."

Then there is the church which, sad to say, has far too long told wounded people that they needed to get over it, get their anger under control, stop having a pity party, or forgive, forget, and move on. We have been taught that the past is the past and we should leave it there, or—my all time favorite—just kill it and let it die.

When that advice was given to me, I wondered, "Kill what? Let what die?" and my very next thought was how I'd like to kill the person who hurt me so badly. I look back now and thank God that I'm not a violent person, because if I were, I might be writing this from my jail cell.

There is always someone waiting to tickle our ears by saying what we want to hear. It can be very confusing trying to figure out which voices to listen to. We get to choose which road we will travel as we try to deal with the pain of our wounds. Will we try to make our wounder pay? Will we decide we are, after all, a victim or a pitiful thing with feelings we shouldn't have? Will we try to just get over it and move on? Will we try to walk away from the past and the pain in our hearts? Will we tolerate the wounds being inflicted on us right now, thinking we deserve them? Will we pretend to be okay and grow a hard heart?

We may try to do what the voices are telling us, believing that we can soothe our pain by getting revenge or that we can pretend the pain isn't there, and all will finally be well with our world. *But this is not only ridiculous, it's a lie to think that we can avenge the wrong done to us, deny our feelings and pain, ignore what is wounding us now, or put the past behind us and, in doing so, make our lives fulfilling and fine.* Life isn't fulfilling when our hearts are hurting, and it isn't good when we are living with unhealed wounds.

But what do you tell people when they ask how you're doing? Do you tell them, "I'm just fine, thank ya ma'am"? That's what we are prone to do. When was the last time you answered honestly, "I'm really hurting. My heart is wounded and I don't know what to do with the pain"?

We are afraid to be truthful because we don't know how others will respond or if they really want to know how we're doing. Frankly, we don't know if we can trust others to protect our hurting hearts.

We live in a world where we are encouraged not to be real but to portray a front that is pleasing to those who see it. We are afraid to be who we really are. I recently read an article in a popular magazine that was about this very issue. It had tips on how to hide everything—extra weight, age indicators, recipes that bombed, personal information, and on and on. There are things in each of our lives that are private. Everyone doesn't need to know the gory details of our lives, but to live hiding who we are and what is going on in our hearts is extremely destructive. It robs us of our very identity.

Because we are afraid to trust others with our hurting hearts, we walk through life being FINE: frustrated, insecure, neurotic, and emotional. We may laugh when we think of it that way, especially if we're women. We blame our FINEness on hormones. We tease and joke with each other, and the men around us seem to find great pleasure in ribbing us about being FINE. They need to take a look in the mirror, though, because men are the same way when they haven't dealt with their wounds. It just plays out differently.

Being FINE—frustrated, insecure, neurotic, and emotional—may be the subject of jokes, but it really isn't funny. We laugh, but this is the reality many of us live in. Our emotions are unpredictable. We have vain imaginations about what others think of us. We are frustrated and angry with ourselves for not just getting over it. Sometimes we feel like we're losing our minds. We find ourselves constantly wondering, "What in the world is wrong with me?"

Many of us with deep wounds have tried so hard to get over it. We've struggled to get our feelings and emotions under control, but because we can't, we end up hiding them, pressing them deeper down inside. We've made an honest effort to forgive the one who wounded us as best we can, but we can't forget. We're trying to move on and put the past back in the past. We're working hard to do what we think we need to do, and we can't understand why our hearts still hurt so badly.

Could it be that we haven't done quite enough? Maybe if we just work harder to push the feelings back where they came from, they will stay there this time. If we pretend that it really didn't happen, maybe the pain will go away. If we can just forget, then we can forgive. If we can stop feeling ashamed, surely we will feel clean again. If we change, maybe our wounder will stop hurting us, and we won't feel guilty any more, and there will be no need to beat *ourselves* up.

Have you ever told yourself any of those things? Many of us tell ourselves at least one of these lies every day. It is interesting that the harder we try to ignore our pain; the deeper we push our feelings down; the more we try to pretend that it didn't happen; the more we make excuses for our response to our pain, the less we are able to control the manifestations of our wounds.

Have you noticed that tendency in yourself? Just when you think you have a handle on the pain, you find yourself bursting into tears for no apparent reason or flying into an angry rage because things didn't go the way you expected. Your mind is flooded with doubts, fears, and insecurities about your worth, your significance, and your abilities. Just when you think you've gotten over it and moved on, you find yourself in another bad relationship, looking for love in all the wrong places. Just when you think the past has finally been banished, it pops up in your present with more fury than before.

We need to stop lying to ourselves, stop making excuses, and get to the root of our bouts with behaviors that are unacceptable, inexplicable, and harmful. These behaviors and reactions that we can't seem to control are neither from some character flaw nor from being "just the way we are."

When you fly off the handle in a fit of anger, there is more to it than a bad temper. When you live in the mire of self-pity, there is more to it than a poor self-image. When you wall off your heart and portray a hard, unfeeling exterior, there is more to it than just being cold and uncaring. When you are submerged in the emotions of depression, you aren't just sad.

You have a wounded heart, a heart that has been broken by the sin of another, your own sin, or the sin of the fallen world we live in. Everything you do to hide your pain, pretend it isn't there, control it, or make excuses for it only deepens your wound and turns your heart and life into a putrid mess.

We all have meltdowns from time to time; that's normal. Some of us have them more frequently and more severely than others. Let me ask you this: When was the last time you had a meltdown that left you asking, "What's wrong with me?" or "Where did that come from?"

Now answer this, do you just brush those questions off or do you think about them until you know the answer? Most of us ask the question and then quickly dismiss it, not realizing how desperately we need to find the answer.

You have to deal with your wounds, not just your feelings toward them. You need to stop being FINE and start being honest. If you don't address the issue of your wounds God's way, you will live the rest of your life as the walking wounded. You will never experience the life that God created you to have. You will live life half dead rather than fully alive.

Reflection & Application

1. What is your greatest fear about sharing your pain?

2. If you have shared your heart pain, what has been the response? How has that response contributed to your healing or to further wounding?

3. Have you tried to "get over it" on your own? How has that worked for you?

Chapter 4

∿

Is That a Wound You're Worshipping?

While we are trying so desperately to move on, get over it, control our emotions, and keep the past in the past, our wounds and the pain they cause gain more and more control over us. They begin to define who we are, how we act, how we interact with others, and even the decisions we make.

We view ourselves in light of our pain and we see the world and our circumstances through it. We relate to others and see their relationship with us through a distorted lens.

Slowly, over time, our wounds become an idol in our lives that we worship. We may not even notice, but we are worshipping them because they have lured us into making them an object of our utmost attention and affection. We bow down to them when we believe things like "this is just who I am," "I can't help the way I act," "I'll never overcome this," "I'll never be able to change," "God has abandoned me," or "no one understands what I'm going through." *As we worship our wounds, we become paralyzed in our pain and we miss the life God desires for us.*

While we're worshipping our wounds we can't really worship God, not the way we are intended to, even when we try. Exodus 20:4 tells us that we are not to bow down to anything but God Himself. Matthew 4:10 says, "Worship the Lord your God and serve him only." God commanded this because He knows that when we try to worship and serve more than one thing at a time, one always wins out and moves to the top of our priority list. Something or someone is always number one in your life and heart.

God is number one simply because He is God, but far too often we want to move God down our list of priorities. We don't seem to understand that He will not settle for being relegated to a spot farther down our lists, even if it's number two. That is why allowing your wound to become an idol in your heart makes your freedom and healing impossible.

You see, when you are living with a broken heart, you are blinded to an essential truth: *You are not the only one who hurts, but God is the only One who heals.* Until you grasp this truth and release your grip on your wound, until you stop bowing down to the pain in your heart and start bowing down to God as your Healer and Deliverer, you will continue to live in the paralysis of your pain.

It is a sad reality that the sin that wounds us and the pain that paralyzes us drives us to sinful thoughts, attitudes, and behaviors that exile us into the bondage of our wound and holds us there. The one who was sinned against becomes the sinner as we desperately try to make sense of our wounds and protect ourselves from more pain. The thoughts, attitudes, and behaviors we engage in may dull the pain of our aching hearts and make us feel protected, but we can't be deceived into believing that dulling of our pain or even the absence of pain justifies our sinful responses. It doesn't mean we are protected or that we are on our way to being okay.

I never thought the shame, guilt, and anger that grew in my heart as a child would continue beyond that part of my life and be unleashed in my adult relationships. I believed that I could keep those feelings and emotions securely where they belonged—in the first eighteen years of my life. But that isn't the way the pain of a wounded heart works.

I don't know what behaviors, attitudes, or thoughts drive you, but I do know that they are part of the grid through which you see the people and circumstances of your life. Your grid is influenced by your own life experiences and it exhibits characteristics that are particular to you.

This is why a rape victim can see every man through the grid of her rapist and not allow another man to get close, but a sexually abused child may grow up to let men use her in the most degrading ways. It explains why a child who can't satisfy the expectations of a parent grows up to be an overachiever, while a child who was spoiled rotten and told she could be anything she wanted to be goes through life with no desire to amount to anything. It allows us to understand why one man whose mother constantly criticized him wants to exert power over women, and another will not step up and take responsibility for leading his family.

For me, every correction I received, every dismissal, every disagreement of opinion left me feeling the same worthlessness and rejection I experienced as a child. I refused to acknowledge the pain and instead protected myself from those childhood feelings by hiding behind my anger and trying to control my world. Some of my siblings felt the same feelings, but went the opposite direction. Rather than lashing out against the pain and protecting themselves, some gave in to the pain and then sought ways to dull it.

Over time the grid through which we view the experiences and people in our lives becomes a stronghold in our hearts. A stronghold is just what it says—it is anything that has a strong enough hold on us that we believe we cannot break free from its grip. When that happens, we are a prisoner to our pain. We have moved from just being burdened by our wound to being in bondage to it with no way out on our own. *Living in the prison of your pain makes you incapable of receiving the words and actions of others at face value.*

How many times has someone said something to you and you found yourself wondering, "What did she mean by that?" "Hmmm, I wonder what they're really trying to tell me."

We may receive a gentle rebuke that is meant to help us, but we feel like we have been sucker punched; or a friend gives us a helpful hint, but what we hear is, "You're too stupid to figure this out for yourself."

Has someone inadvertently done something that upsets you and you know they really didn't mean to, but before you realize it you're convinced that they did it on purpose? You find yourself thinking, "She knew exactly what she was doing! She only did it to make me mad" or "He did that just to upset me and to hurt my feelings."

I remember the panic I used to feel when I would see two strangers talking and then laughing. Immediately I would think, "They're laughing at me." I would give myself a quick once-over to see what was wrong that made them start laughing. Maybe you know that feeling that makes you check to see if there's spinach in your teeth or toilet paper stuck to your shoe.

Have you ever been there? Most of us have. Those responses come from the paralysis of worshipping our wounds, and each time we have one of these episodes our wounds become deeper and more infected.

Writing about this stirs in me such a hatred of sin and Satan, the author of sin. It grieves my heart to see people wasting away in the pain of their wounded hearts, because I have lived there and know the devastation of living in that place. Wounded people are more vulnerable to the attacks of Satan. He knows every breach in the walls of your heart, and he isn't shy about entering those breaches at every opportunity. His sole purpose is to wreak havoc in your life.

John 10:10 tells us that "the thief comes **only** to steal and kill and destroy...."

That is Satan's single-minded objective for you—to kill the essence of who you are, to steal your worth, your joy, your peace, and most of all your hope, and to destroy the person God created you to be.

You were created in the image of God to reflect His character and to worship Him alone, because when we worship Him and Him alone, we experience the life that Jesus came to give us. The rest of John 10:10 says, "… I have come that they may have life, and have it to the full." You are meant to live in the reality of the unique creation that you are. You were created to see yourself in the reflection of Jesus' character and to reflect His character to the world.

Your life is meant to be filled with the love, acceptance, peace, hope, joy, and grace of God.

Ephesians 2:10 says that you are God's masterpiece. Do you see yourself as anyone's masterpiece, let alone God's? God tells us we are a masterpiece, but our broken hearts tell us that we are a piece of junk.

Isaiah 43:4 tells you of God's affection for you, "You are precious and honored in my sight … I love you." Do you feel precious, honored, and loved, or do you feel worthless, rejected, and unloved?

As long as you are worshipping the idol of your broken heart, as long as you are imprisoned in your pain, you will never believe the precious, tender way that God feels toward you. You will never see yourself the way God sees you. You will never know and believe the life-giving, soul-satisfying way that God loves you until you bow down before Him to worship Him alone.

So many people run from God because they don't understand why He allowed them to be wounded. I can't give you an answer to the "why" questions you may be asking. There are things about God that I don't understand either. I only know what God's Word says about this God who sent His only Son so that we could have life, and I have made the choice to believe God's Word.

Deuteronomy 29:29 says, "The secret things belong to the Lord our God."

In Isaiah 55:8, God says, "My thoughts are not your thoughts, neither are your ways my ways." God has ways and purposes that we cannot understand because we aren't God and because we are sinful human beings. We can only see the part of our story that has already been written, but God sees the ending.

If you are weary of living broken, wounded, and in pain, your only hope for freedom and wholeness is to bow your heart before the Lord and choose to believe what His Word says.

Your only hope is to stop worshipping your pain and start worshipping the only One who can heal your wounded heart. When you choose to bow down before Him and ask for His healing, the promise of Jeremiah 29:11-14 is for you:

> "I know the plans I have for you," declares the LORD, "plans to prosper you and not to harm you, plans to give you hope and a future. Then you will call upon me and come and pray to me, and I will listen to you. You will seek me and find me when you seek me with all your heart. I will be found by you," declares the LORD, "and will bring you back from captivity."

God is waiting to release you from the bondage of your wound and unlock the door to whatever prison you have been living in, but you must be a willing participant who will open your heart, look at your wound, and see the reality of what is festering there. God can only call you out of bondage. He can only unlock the prison door. You are the one who has to respond to His call and open the door and walk out of your prison and into the freedom that Christ made possible.

Reflection & Application

1. If you honestly look at the pain in your heart, can you see how that pain has become an idol that has taken God's rightful place? What is the evidence of this in your life?

2. How has your pain paralyzed you? What thoughts, attitudes, and behaviors are keeping you paralyzed in your pain?

3. How has Satan moved into your pain to steal, kill, and destroy you? What has he stolen from you? What parts of your heart feel dead? What has been destroyed in you and your life?

Chapter 5

ॐ

Scabs and Scars

Heart wounds do more than make us feel isolated and alone. They make us feel powerless to change both our situation and ourselves. The longer we worship the idol of our wounds, the more alone and powerless we feel.

Sometimes we *are* powerless to change our situations. Children are the most powerless of all. Where can they turn? If you were abused as a child you need to know that it wasn't your fault. Nothing a child does excuses abuse.

It isn't just children though. Often adults have no idea where to turn for help if they want it. Some really do believe that they are getting what they deserve, that they are somehow provoking the abuse they're suffering.

I remember listening with a sinking heart as a young woman told me that she knew what pushed her abuser's buttons and she just needed to stop pushing them. I was driving at the time and nearly had a wreck when she said that. Anger rose in my heart as I relived memories of my childhood—memories of never entering a room until I'd surveyed the situation and determined who I needed to be and how I needed to act to keep from provoking someone; memories of being made to feel that whatever happened, I had brought it on myself.

Others are so emotionally drained from their pain that they can't think clearly. All they want to do is make it through the day sane and alive. Some live in fear of losing their livelihood or of putting their children or someone else they care about at risk.

Wounds don't always come from parents or spouses, though this is where our thoughts seem to turn first. Some wounds come from work or school or, sadly, even church. We hear stories on the news about kids who are bullied at school and end up killing themselves or someone else. We are all familiar with the stories of sexual abuse by Catholic priests. I remember a story from the newspaper some years ago of the principal at a school for special-needs children spanking his secretary on a regular basis to keep her in line. Can you imagine how demeaning that was to this woman?

These kinds of abuses catch our attention and make us want to scream, "What in the world are they thinking?"

There are other wounds that aren't nearly as visible but nevertheless cause deep pain. To the casual observer the wounding behavior can look benign, but it is a cancer that will spread into the heart of the wounded one causing behaviors that can bring self-inflicted wounds, as well.

These wounds may come from having no rules or boundaries and too much freedom. God created us to have boundary lines. We may enjoy our great freedom, but when there are no guidelines or boundaries, it is confusing and we may wonder if anyone really cares.

I am reminded of a business woman who was given a project to develop, but no guidelines came with it. When she asked for the guidelines she was told if she "was worth her salt" she would figure it out for herself. I listened as she shared her fear and apprehension because she had no idea what her boss was expecting. She worried that her work wouldn't measure up. She doubted her competence to get the job done. Her confidence was shaken because she was given no boundaries within which to do the work. She knew if her work didn't satisfy her boss, she might never move up in her company. She might even lose her job. She worked hard to complete the project and received a "ho-hum" response from her boss. Was this an earth-shattering wound? No, but it was a piece of mortar chipped out of the wall of her heart that damaged her.

I once saw a young man interviewed on a show about family rules. While the other teenagers were complaining about all the rules their parents imposed, this young man shared that he had no curfew, no responsibilities at home, and that his parents didn't get on his case about grades. Just as the other kids started saying how they wished they had his parents, he stopped them and said this: "My parents have a poodle. If that dog gets too near the street, they start screaming for her to come back. If she is hiding in the house, they are frantic to find her. When she is the least bit out of whack, they rush her to the vet. But me, I come and go as I please. Most of the time, they have no idea where I am or even if I am okay. I am sure they love that dog, but I don't know if they really love me."

This young man was wounded by the absence of boundaries that should have been in place to protect him from the frivolous choices that children can make—the often irritating boundaries that tell us that someone cares deeply enough to rein us in.

Other wounding behaviors may appear as concerns for our social acceptance and the development of proper life skills.

I have a dear friend who never was and never will be a girly-girl. However, that didn't sit well with her mother who made her wear frilly dresses, lacey socks, and cutesy shoes. When my friend reached her teens and all her friends wore jeans to youth group, her mother didn't think that was proper church attire, so my friend showed up in a skirt, panty hose, and pumps. She had no interest in singing in the choir, but her mother decided that good little Christian girls did just that. Now you may be thinking that my friend's mother was just teaching her to be feminine or to be a good church member, but what she was doing was denying my friend the opportunity to be the person God created her to be. With every mandate that came down from her mother concerning the way she would dress, the way she would wear her hair, and the way she would act, my friend expressed less and less of her true identity. She knew who she was and how she was wired, but felt that her true self was inadequate because in her mother's eyes it was. Like most every wounded person my friend constructed a survival grid of *self*-wounding behaviors (bad relationships, unwise choices) that allowed her to be who she really was and prove her adequacy.

If we could realize that we are wounding ourselves, we would probably try to stop, but we don't often consider how our behaviors are affecting us personally. Even when we do notice undesirable behaviors in ourselves, we have an uncanny ability to convince ourselves that our behaviors are necessary and therefore, we are okay. While we're telling ourselves these things, Satan is whispering in our ears, "You're right," and sadly we believe him.

We will never get over it, never move on, never be free from our wounds or grow past them until we stop making excuses for our responses and stop pretending that we're okay. Until we start dealing with our wounds and the unhealthy behaviors we have developed in response to our pain, we will continue to deepen our wounds by deceiving ourselves.

If you are going to come out of bondage and into God's freedom, you have to be willing to take a good look at the behaviors you have embraced as a response to your wound. You have to be willing to ask God to search your heart and show you any painful feelings, hurtful attitudes, and sinful responses that you need to bring before Him.

Join David's plea in Psalm 139:23-24, "Search me, O God, and know my heart; test me and know my anxious thoughts. See if there is any offensive way in me, and lead me in the way everlasting."

Nobody enjoys looking at their faults and flaws. It isn't on my list of the top ten things I can't wait to do, but it is absolutely necessary if we are going to experience freedom and healing. You see, even if God zapped each of us right this moment—and that's what we wish He would do, isn't it?—we might be healed from our original wound, but we would still have to deal with the attitudes and behaviors that we have set in motion in an effort to protect ourselves and deny our pain. Without realizing it, we deepen the wound we already have and add to our pain *more* self-inflicted wounds every time we respond to our pain our own way instead of God's way.

Wounded people seem to fall into one of two groups. In keeping with our "wound" theme we will call them "scabs" and "scars." I know you're probably rolling your eyes, but stay with me while I explain.

When I share this, most of you will want to raise your hands and ask, "What if I'm both?" Let me answer that question before you ask—you aren't both. You may have characteristics from both groups, but at your core you are clearly one or the other. I would suggest if you can't figure out which you are, ask those who know you. I can assure you that they have witnessed one trend or the other and have probably had a taste of the fruit it has produced in your life.

These descriptions may seem harsh to you, but if we dance around the truth of who we are, we will never see life-change. We will continue to live in our pain. So please don't take offense. This is not directed at you personally because I don't know you, but it does describe wounded people at the extremes of their pain. Find yourself in one of these profiles, even if the way you have responded isn't quite this dramatic.

Some of you fall into the "scab" category. You see yourself as the victim. Your emotions are dominated by self-pity, which causes you to be on the alert, waiting to be hurt one more time. The least little thing that hurts your feelings prompts your heart to ask, "Why did they hurt me like that?" "Why is everyone against me?" "Why doesn't anyone love me?" In any given situation you feel as though you're getting a raw deal. Your victim mentality makes you feel unworthy to be protected, so you don't even try to protect yourself. You wear your feelings on your sleeve, feeling way too much about most everything. You may burst into tears at the drop of a hat, not because you're tender-hearted and not because you are hurting for someone else, but because you got your feelings hurt once again. You are a "woe is me" person who will tell anyone who will listen the most recent way you have been mistreated. You want people to see your pain and so you find ways to pick at your wound yourself, usually with self-deprecating remarks and questions. "Scabs" often start and end a conversation by saying things like, "I'm so awful" or "I'm just stupid."

They ask questions like "What's wrong with me?" or make declarations of "I can't take it anymore!" or "I just want to die." "Scabs" are waiting to have their wound opened again by an unsuspecting person who just happens to say or do something that knocks the scab off, leaving them to deal with what is festering inside.

You may not be a "scab" yourself, but you recognize the attitudes and behaviors. Maybe you have been in the awkward situation of having said or done something that caused someone to burst into tears or you've seen a smile turn to a pout and you have no idea what's going on. Most of us have been there and it isn't very pleasant, is it?

People who fall into the "scab" group leave us with conflicting feelings—on the one hand we want to give them a big hug and tell them it will be okay and on the other hand we want to run the other way every time we see them coming. We find ourselves involuntarily wondering, "What's it going to be this time?"

"Scars" are polar opposites. Their emotion is anger and, having been in this category myself, I think I can safely say that most of the time this is the only emotion they allow themselves to really feel. "Scars" are survivors who have determined that they will never let anyone hurt them again. However, since that is impossible, when they do feel something akin to pain, they ask, "How dare they do that to me?" "Scars" will protect themselves at all costs, most deliberately by not allowing themselves to feel much of anything about anything. "Scars" have pushed the pain of their wounds deep down inside, out of sight. They won't acknowledge their own wounds or any pain they may cause someone else.

"Scars" have a thick wall built up around their hearts that nothing seems to penetrate, but the reality is that deep below the surface their wounds are causing them bitterness and pain. Any unsuspecting soul who happens to scratch the scar tissue will usually be met with a burst of anger that's been waiting to erupt. We have all been the unsuspecting soul, so it is easy for us to recognize the characteristics of a "scar."

"Scars" are hard people to be around, because we don't feel safe with them. We don't know when the next eruption will come or what will bring it on. If "scars" aren't careful their anger can easily get out of control.

Whether you are a "scab" or a "scar," these responses to the pain of your wounds are selfish and self-focused.

Our wounds keep us from loving and cause us to reject the love of others because we fear being hurt again. I will also say this: It is hard to love "scabs" or "scars" when they are at the extremes of these behaviors.

Both responses are caused by fear. For "scabs" it is the fear of being unloved, unnoticed, and uncared for. It is the fear of fading into the woodwork and never really being seen for who they are. Their greatest fear is not being known and not being loved. They act out in ways that assure they are noticed, hoping that this will bring them love, tenderness, and compassion.

"Scars" live with the fear of exposure and losing control. They don't allow themselves to feel because their feelings are unpredictable. "Scars" keep a tight rein on their emotions and their environment. They usually don't see their outbursts of anger as losing control because, after all, the person (or situation) that caused the outburst deserved it. A "scar's" greatest fear is being seen as weak or not in control of themselves or their circumstances. Looking back, I have to shake my head and smile because nothing seems weaker or more out of control to me now than a person who is spewing anger. "Scars" are extremely insecure people. Though they may appear tough and overly confident, "scars" hide their insecurities by diminishing others through harsh criticism, snide sarcasm, or degrading humor.

Let's have an honest moment here: When we witness these behaviors in others, we often wonder why these people don't just stop acting that way, don't we? When we have a lucid moment that lets us see these behaviors in ourselves, we kick ourselves in the rear asking why we can't just change. We see others and ourselves as stuck.

I have many opportunities to identify with Paul's lament in Romans 7:15, "I do not understand what I do. For what I want to do I do not do, but what I hate I do." How about you? Do you feel stuck in the repetition of doing what you don't want to do or feeling helpless to act in the way you do want to act? Do you ever have "grrrrr" moments, because you have blown it once again?

If you feel this way, take heart, there is hope. Paul goes on to say in Romans 7:17-18, "As it is, it is no longer I myself who do it, but it is sin living in me. I know that nothing good lives in me, that is, in my sinful nature. For I have the desire to do what is good, but I cannot carry it out."

We are only stuck if we choose to be. The hope of being unstuck isn't in anything we can do for ourselves, but there is hope for anyone who will take these two verses to heart. Sin lives in us, and God is only one who can do anything about our wound or our sin. The truth is that we are stuck because we're sinful and because nothing good lives in us, and we will stay stuck as long as we try to get over it our way in our own strength.

When you feel alone and stuck in the pain of your wounded heart you have to believe that God is the only one who fully understands your pain and that He knows what you need to do to get unstuck. If you have tried to get over your wound and your pain and your best efforts have failed; if you have given up, believing that your destiny is to live the rest of your life in the pain of your wounds; if you believe that everyone else can get over it but not you, here is the truth you can cling to:

God has the way already in place to get you unstuck, and His way is the only way that works.

In Him you will find everything you need to get over it because you *do need* to get over it, but you need to do it God's way.

Reflection & Application

1. It is time to ask God to search your heart and show you the ways that you are deceiving yourself. Will you take time to sit quietly, ask Him to reveal your heart to you, and listen and record what He shows you?

2. Are you a "scab" or a "scar?" How do you see this manifested in your attitudes, words, and behaviors?

3. Do you feel stuck in your woundedness and pain? How will it change you and your life if you choose to believe that God can get you unstuck?

Chapter 6

☙

No More Masks

The wounds of a broken heart are like any other kinds of wounds. If they're not tended they become infected. Heart wounds worsen with reminders of the wrong that hurt us and all the emotions that follow, but they also conjure up vain imaginations and lying accusations that fill us with shame and guilt. The pain of a wounded heart and the accompanying losses can overwhelm us, consume our thoughts, and drive our attitudes and behaviors.

In the 10th grade, my best friend caught her boyfriend kissing one of our other friends behind the bleachers at a football game. Bleachers ... they always seem to be getting someone in trouble, don't they?

My friend's heart was broken, and the wound it left did double duty on her. Not only did her boyfriend cheat on her, but a friend betrayed her. For weeks I patiently listened minute after minute, hour after hour, day after day as she mourned in her all-consuming pain. Everything, even the sandwich she brought for lunch, somehow reminded her of "him." I tried to console her, but she would tell me that I just didn't understand and there was no way she would ever get over it. Her heart was broken, plain and simple.

As the year passed and summer arrived, we laughed about all the drama. She thought she was finally over it, but she wasn't. I noticed that after that heartbreak and betrayal she was always a little suspicious of people, especially the guys she dated. She had been wounded, and though the pain of that wound was gone, she was missing the piece of her heart called trust.

As I write these words, a precious friend is mourning the loss of her husband to pancreatic cancer. She has been so honest and open in her journey of aloneness. She shares the pain of answering the phone expecting to hear his voice, of getting ready to prepare dinner so he can eat when he gets home. She recently flew to another state to visit her sister and got off the plane thinking she should call the love of her life to tell him she'd arrived safely. My friend has openly shared questioning things she has believed all her life, trying to figure out if she still believes them now that her heart has been yanked out of her chest. She can't get her mind off of the pain right now. Her heart is a gaping wound and everything reminds her of her loss.

That is what the ugliness of the wounds of sin does to us. If sin had not entered the world, there would be no death, no disease, no betrayal, no pain! But sin did enter and now we are left to deal with its destruction.

I don't understand how we can be so passive about dealing with our own heart wounds. If we would just make ourselves look at the destruction that our wounds have caused in us, we would not be passive. If we would look objectively at the continuing damage done by our protective measures and survival grids, I believe we would stop using them to numb our pain, and we could move into decisive action to find healing and freedom. If we understood the depth of God's love for us and how desperately He desires for us to experience the abundant life Christ came to give, surely we would passionately pursue God and His plan for us. If we had a clear picture of the "me" that God intended, the "me" that is created in His image to reflect His glory, I believe that with all of our might we would push through the obstacles that are keeping us from being the person God created us to be.

But more often than not, we are blind to the damage our heart wounds have done to the "me" that should be; or in our pain we are indifferent to the damage we are doing to the hearts of others. Even when we catch a glimpse of the damage, we are apt to allow fear or pride to keep us paralyzed in our pain.

We seem to think that the pain will somehow go away on its own. You've heard the saying "time heals all wounds." That's what we think, but that simply isn't true. Time allows our wounds to grow and eat away at us, but it also allows us to ignore the pain long enough to learn to live with it.

If enough time goes by, our pain begins to feel like just a dull ache that we convince ourselves we have to endure as a normal part of life.

We are passive about our own wounds, but we are often callous with others who are suffering from the pain of a wounded heart. Some of us want to step into the pain of others, but we have no idea how to help them because we can't even seem to help ourselves. We don't know how to just be present with others who are hurting. We feel like we should offer words of wisdom or answers for their pain, but when we have none, we are prone to walk away and leave others alone with their wounds.

There are some, though, who never even approach another who is suffering with the pain of a wounded heart. These are people who feel extremely uncomfortable in the presence of those who are hurting. Often these people find themselves wishing the other person would just get over it. They want to put a time limit on how long people are allowed to be in pain. They wonder why hurting people can't just put it all behind them and move on with their lives.

This is where I should be able to say to you, "Join me; do what I am doing; stop being passive about your own pain. Do whatever you have to do to be the 'you' that God created you to be; let God heal you and set you free. Don't be callous with others who are hurting; don't let their pain make you so uncomfortable that you leave them to wallow in it all alone. Be willing to just be present with another whose heart is wounded; be patient; let them be healed and free on God's timetable, not man's!"

But I must confess that I am guilty of being passive and callous at times, and I don't like that about myself. As far as I have come on my journey into God's freedom and healing, I still am not at my journey's end and probably never will be. Sin, my own and that of others, will continue to wound me, and each time I will have to make a choice to either deal with it decisively God's way or to move passively into my self-protective mode.

If our wounds or the wounds of others were physical and visible, we would have a very different response. We would pay attention and take action. We would not be passive or callous.

If you had a gaping, infected wound on your leg you wouldn't ignore it or live with it. The people in your life wouldn't tell you to put it behind you and move on. No one would make you feel like you should just get over it, nor would you feel guilty and ashamed for feeling the pain.

Our wounds, whether physical or emotional, need the care of someone who can see what's growing there and do what needs to be done to stop the spread of the infection; and believe me, the process can be very painful. I'm sorry to be so graphic, but we need someone to scrape out the pus, cut away the scar tissue, and close up our wound so it can heal properly.

Jesus is our someone, and He is our only someone.

Isaiah 61:1-2 says this of Jesus, "The Spirit of the Sovereign Lord is on me, because the Lord has anointed me to preach good news to the poor. He has sent me to bind up the brokenhearted, to proclaim freedom for the captives and release from darkness for the prisoners."

Do you see what Jesus came to do for you? The Hebrew word for "bind up" paints a word picture of God taking your heart in His hands and applying pressure until the bleeding stops. Imagine that, the loving hands of your compassionate, heavenly Father wrapped gently around your hurting heart.

What a precious, tender picture of how God cares for those whose hearts have been wounded by sin. As the pressure God applies stops the bleeding of your wounded heart, something else happens, too. It squeezes out the painful feelings, hurtful attitudes, and sinful responses that you need to bring to Him.

Jesus came to call you out of the bondage of your wounded heart. He has no desire for you to be held captive by it any longer. He came to release you from the darkness that surrounds the life of all who are living in the pain of their wounds. He came, too, to set you free from the prison of your own response to your wounded heart.

Jesus came! Think about that. God could have chosen to zap us from afar with healing and freedom. Jesus did not have to come. He could have stayed in heaven and done it all. But He chose instead to come down to us. My mind can hardly imagine that Almighty God stayed confine in Mary's womb for nine months and then lived on this earth to experience the same criticism, rejection, cruelty, suffering, humiliation, and pain that we do.

My sin, your sin, and the sin of others that wounds your heart and mine nailed Jesus, sinless Jesus, to the cross and it held Him there until our freedom and healing were secured.

Jesus' love for mankind and His hatred of sin and what it does to us compelled Him to suffer and die on the cross and then to rise victoriously from the grave so that we can be free from the bondage of our wounds and the pain they cause.

You may be living in circumstances right now that are tearing your heart apart:

You may be going through a divorce or trying desperately to make a bad marriage work.

It could be that there is an abusive person in your life—a spouse, a parent, a friend, or even a boss.

You may be living with the heartache of a rebellious child who has walked away from everything you taught and seems intent on ruining his or her life. You may feel powerless to do anything to influence or help the situation.

Maybe you have suffered the recent death of a loved one and you don't know how you will go on without them or if you even want to go on.

Some of you have suffered the betrayal of a friend or the loss of a job or a home or something else that you held dear.

Whatever your wound, it is fresh and the pain is intense, and you know that your life has been changed forever.

Your wound may have been festering for years. It may be the nagging pain of a small wound or the unbearable pain of a huge wound that is robbing you of life.

Have you endured physical, mental, sexual, or emotional abuse? Do you live with the shame, guilt, suspicion, and fear that this abuse brings?

Did your parents divorce when you were young and tear your world apart?

Could it be that you had an absent parent and the absence made you feel insignificant and unimportant?

Were you bullied at school or the object of ridicule or jokes?

You may have a learning disability that has always made you feel dumb.

Maybe you aren't the prettiest sister or the smartest child in the family and no one ever told you that, but they let you know in inadvertent ways with disapproving looks or subtle remarks made to your face or behind your back.

It could be that no matter how hard you tried, you could never live up to the expectations of a significant person in your life, and so you lived with criticism and rejection at every turn.

You may have a physical or medical condition that makes you the "different" one, or the one who was excluded from activities by necessity or someone else's choice.

For years you may have been living with the effects of the cruelty of a circumstance or person that was totally out of your control.

It may be that your wound has been passed down to you from wounded grandparents or parents. There are people who have had the same wound in their family for generations: addictions, abuse, or character flaws such as lying, cheating, or stealing. Generational wounds are behaviors that may seem normal to us because they are so familiar. Our conscience may break through from time to time and tell us our behavior is wrong, but we excuse it because it has been part of our lives for so long.

I grew up in a home where lying was a means to an end. I wasn't told that lying was okay, but what was modeled to me was that it was acceptable if it achieved the desired result. I moved into adulthood thinking that lying was okay if there was a "legitimate" reason to stretch the truth or even tell an outright lie. Lying was a character flaw I had to overcome in God's power. From the time I was a small child I felt the guilt of even the smallest stretch of the truth. I knew the uncertainty of not knowing whether I was being told the truth or not. I figured if I lied then so did everyone else. When I got married I wanted to trust and be trusted, and when I became a mom I didn't want my children to live like I did with questions in their minds when I told them something.

I had to choose to stop the cycle of the generational sin that wounded my heart and influenced my life. If I didn't stop it, I knew I ran the risk of that character flaw being passed down to my children.

Any wound you have has the potential to be passed down to the next generation. It may not be the same thing that wounded you, but behaviors you put in place to deal with your pain can certainly be passed down to your children and even your grandchildren.

Only when you allow Jesus to bind up your broken heart and set you free from the prison of your pain can you ensure that you will either break or prevent the cycle of generational sin. If you don't allow Jesus to set you free, your response to your wounds may become a generational sin that is passed on through you.

Sin and its wounds are no respecters of persons, position, or power. They did not even bypass the sinless Son of God.

Isaiah 53:5 says that "He [Jesus] was pierced for our transgressions, he was crushed for our iniquities; the punishment that brought us peace was upon him, and by his wounds we are healed."

Whatever your wound, you have been exiled into bondage by it, and Jesus Christ suffered and died on the cross—He was wounded in terrible ways—so that you can be healed. *He is the only one who truly understands your pain. Jesus Christ is the only one who can heal your wounds.*

Until you grab hold of these truths and claim them as your own, you will stay under the control of your wounds. You will continue to bow down and worship the idol of your pain by deceiving yourself into believing you are okay and telling yourself that you have overcome and moved on. Or you will convince yourself that you will never be okay and so there is no need to try to move forward.

You will continue to be wounded, not necessarily by your original wound, but by the behaviors, protective measures, and survival grid that you have put in place to take your mind off the pain in your heart.

You are the only one who knows the things that are continually wounding you; and if you don't, God is waiting to show you if you will ask Him. Until you identify the coping mechanisms you have put in place and face the reality that they are only masking your wound and its pain, you will live with your facade firmly in place. You will live in deception while your wounded heart drains all hope and joy from your life.

It takes so much emotional energy to pretend that all is well when it's not. Pretending fills our hearts with the fear of being discovered and exposed. Living behind our masks keeps us constantly on our guard lest our masks should slip even a little and allow others to see what is really in our hearts and our lives.

A life of pretense always holds us in bondage because we're living a lie.

My coping mechanisms went into place when I was a young girl. As a child I really did have to pretend that everything was fine just to protect myself because showing emotion or questioning what went on in our home could bring severe consequences. I convinced myself that if I was attentive enough to my surroundings, if I learned to read the moods and temperaments of others and adjusted my actions accordingly, then I wouldn't be hurt. I learned to become whoever I needed to be at just the right time in order to stay safe. I settled for playing the part that was expected of me, and I actually became a pretty good actress, convincing myself that I could survive anything if I just played my part right.

I'm not sure when I started believing that all was okay, but at some point my pretense became my reality. I lived behind my carefully constructed facade for so many years that by the time I left home and went to college, I had no idea who I really was. I had played so many different parts in the first eighteen years of my life that I didn't believe I would ever know the real me.

I wanted to find myself, to stop acting in order to protect myself, and to drop the pretense; but frankly, I was afraid of who I would find behind the facade. I was afraid that the person I found there, the real me, would be weak and unable to cope and survive on her own.

It wasn't until I let God show me who the real me was that I understood I wasn't the one who was keeping me safe, and I wasn't the one protecting myself. I may have lived through my childhood, but I was not the survivor I thought I was. The whole time I was depending on myself for protection and safety, I was adding my own *self*-inflicted wounds to the wounds that came from my parents.

What I found behind my facade was an eighteen-year-old little girl who had grown cold, angry, and afraid of loving and being loved. I found an adult with a rock hard exterior who was emotionally stunted, insecure, and in deep pain. I didn't like the real person I found and fought hard to put her back where she came from, but I had tasted the freedom of being real—no matter how undesirable "real" was—and my heart wouldn't let me go back.

God wants to bring you out of bondage and into His freedom and healing, but that isn't going to happen as long as you are being wounded again and again by the coping mechanisms that you have put in place. *Your only hope for freedom and healing is to drop the facades and defenses, take off the masks you have been wearing, and look in the mirror to see who you really are.*

Satan does not want you free or healed, so he will convince you that you are only protecting yourself from the judgment of others or from being misunderstood. He will tell you that if you drop your defenses you will be hurt again. Satan wants you to believe that you can't trust anyone with your hurting heart, especially God. "After all," he will ask you, "where was God when you were being hurt? If God didn't protect you then, what makes you think He will protect you now?" Have you heard Satan whispering his lies in your ear? Have you accepted his lies as the truth?

If you have, it's time for you to call them what they are—LIES—because as long as you believe he is telling you the truth, as long as you keep your defenses firmly in place, you will stay stuck right where you are, living imprisoned in the pain of your wounded heart. God's truth is the only thing that can push aside the lies, masks, facades, and defense mechanisms that are keeping you stuck in your pain.

It's time for you to take off your masks, drop your defenses, and trust in something besides yourself. God's love, mercy, and grace will get you unstuck. They are your only hope!

Reflection & Application

1. When you think about the "me" God created you to be, who do you see? Describe that person. Do you like what you see?

2. In what ways are you passive about your wounds and the pain they have caused?

3. What are the coping mechanisms and masks that you have put in place to deal with the pain in your heart?

Chapter 7

∿

Hope Gives Life

Hope is powerful. Webster defines hope as "desire accompanied by anticipation and expectation." Proverbs 13:12 says, "Hope deferred makes the heart sick," and medical doctors tell us that without hope a person loses the will to live. Imagine that. Hope is so powerful that it determines not only the health of your heart but whether you and I will desire to go on living or give up on life altogether.

We all hope for something and hope in something.

So when it comes to your wounded heart, you have two very important questions to answer: What are you hoping *for*? And what are you hoping *in*?

The outcome of your journey toward freedom and healing depends on your answering both of these questions honestly, from the heart. Take some time to think about what you anticipate and expect healing to look like in your life. What is it you hope for?

Do you hope for the one who wounded you to pay for how they hurt you? Do you want them to suffer as much as you have? Or do you hope they suffer more? Maybe you'd like to see them pay with their life. Many people believe that if the other person pays for what they did, there will be closure and healing. They believe that life cannot go on until that happens.

Do you hope for the relationship with your wounder to be restored? I talk with people all the time who honestly believe that if their wounder will acknowledge what they've done, say they're sorry, and ask for forgiveness, healing will be almost instantaneous.

Do you hope for an opportunity to let the one who wounded you see the depth of pain they've caused? You may believe that freedom and healing will come if you can just communicate how deeply you were wounded and how severely you suffer. You may be tired of holding the pain inside or afraid to speak your mind, but you really believe that if you can share your heart and get the emotions and pain off your chest, then the one who wounded you will surely understand how much pain and destruction they've caused in your life. You believe that when that happens you will be free to move forward.

Could it be that you hope for the chance to hurt your wounder back by unleashing your anger and wrath on them? Do you want to wound them in the same way they wounded you? Do you daydream about how great it will feel to see them hurt like you hurt?

Do you hope for the strength to just walk away from the pain, to put it all behind you, to forget, and never have to think about the pain or what caused it again? Your hope may be to never have to deal with what or who wounded you. You have no desire to face your wounder or speak your mind or make them pay. You just want to move on and have a normal life.

As you hope for whatever it is that you believe will bring freedom and healing to your heart, you have to identify what or who you are hoping in to bring the expected outcome. What do you hope in?

Do you hope in some form of justice to make your wounder pay? Do you hope in your own ability to bring justice to your situation? Do you hope in the power of closure to give you back your life?

Do hope in the healing power of words of regret and humility from another person? Do you hope in the restoration of a relationship to also restore all that was lost?

Do you hope in the desire of your wounder to see the pain they have caused and have compassion for you? Do you hope in your own ability to make them understand what they have done and how wrong it was?

Maybe you hope in the power of your anger to exact the revenge of pain? You may hope, as well, in your belief that healing for your own heart is found in destroying the heart of the one who caused you pain.

Is your hope in your own strength to forget the pain and its source, to live as though it never happened, and to prove that you can move on with your life?

I have hoped in and hoped for every one of these things. *I moved from one to the other looking for the one thing that would satisfy my hope and not disappoint me.* Others have tried even more desperately than I did to dull their pain and find hope in one thing or another.

I have seen wives whose husbands have betrayed them cry in anguish, "He won't get away with this!" and then watched as they used their divorce attorney to ruin the business, reputation, or life that their husband worked so hard to build.

Mothers and fathers destroy their children in an effort to hurt their spouse more than their spouse hurt them. Some do this through lies that tear the other person down, others through false accusations. Some are more subtle, making excuses for the parent with well-chosen words that leave a question in the child's mind of whether their mother or father really loves and cares for them.

An adult child may go time and time again to an abusive parent sharing her (his) pain, explaining how the pain of abuse has defined her (his) life, asking directly or indirectly, "Do you love me? Do you care?"

As one woman told me, "I have given my father one opportunity after another to ask for my forgiveness, and he just doesn't get it."

Therein lies the problem: Those who wound us are just like we are when we unconsciously wound others. They don't understand the gravity of their words or actions! Many times those who wound us think, at least at the time, that what they are doing is being done in love for our good.

Abusive people don't get it! They call physical abuse *discipline*, emotional abuse *helpful instruction*, and sexual abuse *loving*. Most of us have watched TV in horror as a pedophile declares his love for the children whose lives he has ruined. We have heard of abusive husbands saying they are just trying to make their wives the best they can be, or abusive parents declaring they want to keep their kids on the right track or teach them a lesson.

Those who wound with critical remarks or shame-producing admonition don't get it! They really do believe that the one they unleash their words upon will change his or her behavior. My father honestly believed that withholding words of encouragement and pointing out only what was flawed would produce excellence in me and my siblings. Teachers, parents, employers, and others often believe that causing a person public shame will make them stop their "unacceptable" behavior.

Because my most poignant response to my pain was anger, I can tell you without hesitation that I suffered more internalized pain and destruction from my anger than I could ever have brought to the ones who hurt me. Like others who hope in their anger, my anger was eating away at my heart. While those who were the object of my anger and bitterness went on with their lives and hearts intact, I was paralyzed in the pain of my wound and in the destruction of my anger.

You and I both know men and women who run from their pain or their past through accomplishments, prestige, and power. People all around us use these things to prove to themselves and others that they *do* have worth, even if their parents, siblings, friends, or teachers can't see it. People work with all their might to rise above social stigmas, financial deficiencies, physical inadequacies, or other things that label them as less significant. With every degree or additional letter that goes behind their name, with every promotion or pay raise, with every award or public acknowledgment, some are still running as hard as possible from whatever or whoever wounded them.

There is a problem with the things that we hope for and hope in. They bring only momentary pleasure and satisfaction. Every one of these things requires more and more of the same to keep the satisfaction coming. The hope we seek through our own desires and efforts will always disappoint us. If you're honest you'll admit that what you thought would bring an end to your pain, what you thought would make it possible for you to move on or get over it, what you thought would make you feel worthwhile and important, what you thought would give you a normal life, what you hoped in and hoped for has left you feeling empty and unsatisfied.

The key to a hope that does not disappoint is that the object of your hope is worthy of your trust. When we have disappointed ourselves and been disappointed by others, we have to wise up. We have to learn that anything we do and anything we expect from others will always leave us wanting. We need to look somewhere else for our hope, because we cannot trust in ourselves or others for the freedom and healing we desire.

You have only one hope, and your hope has a name. His name is Jesus. First Timothy 1:1 tells us that Christ Jesus is our hope. He is our hope for every need that we have. Jesus came to bind up our broken heart. He came to set us free and heal our wounds. He came to release us from the darkness of the prison of our pain. But He also came to do much more. He came to give us *hope* for a future after the pain is gone, after our heart is healed, and after we are set free.

A healed heart is a heart without a wound or its pain. Freedom is being out of bondage. But we need more than just freedom and healing. We need life, and freedom and healing *with hope* is life!

Don't you want life? I do! I want to be truly living, not just existing from one day to the next, but I know that for me to truly live, my hope has to be in the right place, in Jesus Christ. If you want life, your hope must be in Jesus, too. You have to believe that nothing you do on your own and nothing your wounder does to make amends will ever set you free or heal your heart. Jesus came to do that for you. He died on the cross so that "by His wounds you are healed" (Isaiah 53:5) because He is the only One who can heal you. You and your wounder can contribute to the healing process, but only Jesus can heal a heart and set it free.

For you to believe in Jesus as your only hope there is another issue you must settle. I am convinced that the greatest struggle for all mankind is believing that Jesus loves us, truly loves us as individuals. We may believe that God loves the world as John 3:16 says, but it is so hard for us to personalize His love with unwavering assurance. For you to live in the hope that only comes from Jesus, you have to be able to look in the mirror and say with conviction, "Jesus loves me."

I'm not talking about, "Jesus loves me this I know for the Bible tells me so." Believing that Jesus loves you because the Bible says so *can* be a mere intellectual exercise. You can know it in your head, but I'm talking about knowing in your heart that Jesus loves you—period—with no qualifiers attached. You have to know-that-you-know-that-you-know that Jesus loves you no matter what you do or don't do, no matter who you are or are not, no matter what you say or don't say, no matter what you think or don't think, and no matter what you believe or don't believe.

You see, whether you believe it or not doesn't change the fact that Jesus loves you!

It took me years to finally believe that Jesus loves me, and not only loves me, but He loves me so much that He came to this earth and suffered and died just to save me. For the first fifteen years of my Christian life I doubted Christ's love for me. Because I wasn't sure of His love, I didn't fully trust Him to protect me, provide for me, listen to me, answer my prayers, take care of my family, heal me, or set my heart free.

I wasn't just living in the prison of my pain. I was living in the prison of my unbelief.

Nineteen eighty-five was not a good year for me to be struggling with unbelief. We were staff members of Campus Crusade for Christ and had just returned to the United States after five years in the Philippines. We were still in the process of moving to Arkansas when we were surprised to learn that we were pregnant with our third child. Our son was born one month after we moved into our new home, and for the first time I struggled with post-partum depression. If you've never experienced it, let me assure you—it's the pits!

When our son was two months old, my husband had to go out of town for ten days and, as life would have it, the day after he left I got sick with strep throat. I was sicker than I ever remember being and the only two people I knew well enough to call for help were both out of town as well. Lying on my bed with post-partum depression, strep throat, a fever of 104, a nursing baby, an eight-year-old, a four-year-old, and a husband out of town sent me into a crisis of belief that lasted for almost three months.

During that time I wrestled with God over the entirety of my life. I asked all of the why questions, the how-could-you questions, and the is-it-just-me questions. I couldn't bring myself to conclude that God just outright didn't love me, but I was sure at the time that He didn't love me as much as He loved everyone else.

As it turned out, however, this was to be one of the best years of my life. You see, I am as stubborn as a mule, and I couldn't let it go. I had to have the answers to all of my questions, so I hounded God, asking the questions over and over again.

I still remember that day. The two older children were at school and the baby was sleeping. I was sitting in the middle of my bed pleading with God, once again, to tell me what was wrong with me that kept Him from really loving me. I wanted to know what I needed to do to make Him love me as much as He loved everyone else. In that moment God did for me what I couldn't do for myself—He wrote on my heart that He loved me with all of His heart! You see, God knew I had no context for understanding a father's love. He knew I would never embrace the depths of His love on my own, so as I sat there on my bed crying out to Him, God graciously granted me the faith to believe that His great love abounded toward me. God helped me believe what He said to me in Isaiah 43:4, "You are precious and honored in my sight, and … I love you." He showed me the depth of His love for me in Jesus' words in John 15:9, "As the Father has loved me, so have I loved you. Now remain in my love." As hard as it was for me to fathom that Jesus loves me just as much as God the Father loves God the Son, my heart could not resist being loved so deeply and so passionately. God granted me the gift of faith that day to plant my heart in the soil of His love and allow it to take root and grow there.

Believing in the depths of your heart that Jesus loves you ignites in your heart the faith to trust Him to be your only hope.

You and I will never fully trust anyone, God or man, if we don't believe they truly love us. We will never place our pain and our brokenness securely in the hands of someone whose love we question and doubt. That is why you must settle this issue in your own heart if you are going to walk with God into healing and freedom.

Faith in God's love for you and His plan for your life opens the door for you to walk out of the bondage of your wounded heart.

If you struggle to believe that God loves you to pieces, wrestle with Him over this issue. He will not let you down. He will meet you at your point of need, and if your heart's desire is to believe the truth of God's amazing love for you, He will show His love in a way that opens the eyes of your heart to see and believe.

Jesus is your hope for freedom and healing, your only hope. He came to step into your woundedness and replace your pain with life, but your hope for life is only possible when you place your faith in Him.

Hebrews 11:1 says that "faith is being sure of what we hope for and certain of what we do not see." You can be certain that if you hope in Jesus Christ, you will one day see the pain of your broken heart replaced with God's freedom and healing.

Reflection & Application

1. List the things that you hope for and hope in when it comes to your wounds and the pain they have caused you.

2. Do you believe in your heart that Jesus loves you, really loves you? If you struggle with believing that Jesus loves you, can you put into word's why?

3. What difference would it make in your life and your healing process if you could plant your heart in the soil of God's love and let it take root and grow there?

Chapter 8

∾

Life, It's Yours for the Taking

Jesus came to bind up your broken heart and bring you out of the bondage of your pain and into His freedom. The freedom and healing that comes from Jesus Christ is meant to usher you into an intimate relationship with God that releases you to worship Him with all of your being, and in doing so to find the life that you desire and the person that you were meant to be before sin wounded your heart.

God sets us free to stay free. Galatians 5:1(NASB) tells us: "It is for freedom that Christ has set us free; therefore keep standing firm and do not be subject again to a yoke of slavery."

God's plan is for us to come out of the bondage of sin that wounds us and remain in His freedom; but rather than living fully in God's freedom, we seem to live our lives wandering back and forth between the freedom Christ has given us and the bondage of the wounds that sin inflicts on our hearts.

If you are going to keep standing firm in your freedom and healing and not return to the bondage of your wounds, you have to know how that happens.

It surely doesn't happen when others tell you to move on, get over it, let it go, walk away from the past and leave it behind, or simply forgive and forget.

Your efforts to "stand firm" in those ways only dull your pain and deny its cause. I don't see any scriptural basis for doing that or for anyone setting a limit on the time you have to plant your feet firmly in the freedom of Christ. But neither do I see that you and I have permission to wallow in our wounds and pain or use them as an excuse for all that is wrong in our lives.

God wants to bring us out of the bondage of our wounds. The death and resurrection of Jesus Christ paved the way for all who will place their faith and hope in Him. God really doesn't want us FINE (frustrated, insecure, neurotic, and emotional). He wants us free from the idols that our wounds have become, free from the grip of the pain in our hearts, free from the protective measures we have put in place, and free from the hurtful attitudes and sinful responses that have grown from our unhealed wounds.

God wants us free from anything that keeps us from being wholly His. *How can we be wholly His when we are not whole?* We can't. And we would be in a hopeless and forsaken place if God didn't have a plan for our wholeness.

I love God's Word, because it has the answers to all of life's issues, even the pain of our wounds. It shows us a process that lets us partner with God so that we can work together with Him toward wholeness.

Remember Isaiah 61:1-2? It tells us that Jesus came to bind up the brokenhearted, to preach good news to the poor, to proclaim freedom for the captives, and release from darkness for the prisoners. This is what Christ offers to you when your heart has been broken by the wounds of sin and you are living in captivity to your wounds, imprisoned in your pain. *The good news for you is that because God wants you healed and free, He will lead you there if you will let Him.*

God always does what He promises, but we have a responsibility to work with Him and cooperate with Him until the process is complete.

Isaiah 61 goes on to say in verse 4: "They will rebuild the ancient ruins and restore the places long devastated; they will renew the ruined cities that have been devastated for generations."

God's process is right there. Do you see your part? God will bring freedom and healing so that *you* can work with Him to rebuild, restore, and renew the devastated and ruined places of your own heart.

We all want healing for our heart wounds. We want the pain to go away. We want to be free from the destruction that our wounded hearts have caused, don't we? And praise God! He will heal us and set us free, but we can't stop there. We must work to be whole, so that we can be wholly His.

When God has your whole heart, then you can stand firm in your freedom and never be in bondage to the pain of woundedness again.

The question for you is this, "When God heals you, will you rebuild what sin has torn down?"

When we are healed, but not rebuilt it is like having an amputated body part. The wound from the amputation may be healed well enough for the pain to be gone, but the part is still missing. The wound is healed, but the amputee is disabled, because she isn't whole. To be whole she needs that part, so what does she do? She replaces the missing part with a prosthesis when needed but takes it off when it's not needed.

We can let God heal our wounded hearts, we can forgive the one who wounded us, and we can be living without the pain we once felt very deeply, but we can still be missing a huge part of our hearts.

For years I lived healed, but I was incapacitated by the pieces of my heart that were still missing. My parents had stolen my innocence, my childhood, my self-confidence, my security, and my ability to feel safe. They did not value me as a unique person. I was insecure in relationships—as much as my sweet husband loved me and showed it, I found myself doubting his love. I didn't trust anyone and was suspicious of everyone. I was unsure of myself, even in the areas of my greatest strengths. I was afraid to try new things, so my life became a rut of walking in only the familiar. Part of that stemmed from expecting myself to fail because my dad told me I would never amount to anything. I didn't try because I didn't want to prove my father right. I felt insignificant to everyone, especially God, so I was not able to reach the full potential for which I was created. Because I was missing parts of my heart, I couldn't function and flourish as fully as I was designed to.

When the pain was gone, my life was totally different. God had opened the door of my prison cell and I was free. I had opened my hand and released the anger that held both my parents and me hostage. God had healed my wound, but there was still work to be done to put the missing pieces of my heart back together.

Trying to live without a whole heart is like trying to sew with a sewing machine that has no thread or needle. The machine works, but it can't do what it was designed to do because it is missing something essential.

I did just what an amputee does. In public I put on whatever I needed to compensate for the parts of my heart that were missing—I plastered on my prosthetic smile and my prosthetic air of confidence and self-assurance. I learned to use my prosthetics well enough that others had no idea that I was missing huge parts of myself, but when I was at home the prosthetics came off.

When I trusted God to heal my wound, I felt the pain go. My heart felt free, but my self-confidence, sense of security, innocence, and worth as a person did not come tumbling back into my heart. My fear of failure and rejection did not instantly go away. Those all had to be restored as I rebuilt my heart with God.

God promises in Joel 2:25 (AMP), "I will restore or replace for you the years that the locust have eaten." He promises to restore what has been stolen from us in our woundedness. God doesn't just want to take away the pain in your heart; He wants to put your broken heart back together.

I knew what had been stolen from me and I wanted it back, but *I wasn't sure I trusted God enough to believe that He would put my heart back together, and I was scared to death of what my rebuilt life would look like.* I know that sounds silly, but I knew how to live life with my brokenness.

Remember the survival grid, the masks, the facade, and the protective measures? Mine were firmly in place, and I was sure that removing them would not be a pleasant process. Why would I want to add unpleasantness to my brokenness and bring pain on myself? I was comfortable as I was. I was comfortable, but not content, not fulfilled, and not satisfied. Before I inflicted more pain on myself, I needed an answer to this question, "Does God love me enough to be kind, patient, and tender with me as we rebuilt my heart together?"

God answered that question for me and for you in Jeremiah 31:3-4a (NASB), "I have loved you with an everlasting love; therefore I have drawn you with loving-kindness. Again I will build you, and you shall be rebuilt."

Do you see that? God's love for you and me is everlasting. It is solid as a rock. His love won't ever change or be withdrawn. He draws us to Himself, not with force or roughness, but with loving-kindness, so that He can put us back together the way He intended for us to be before sin moved in with its destructive force.

God wants you rebuilt, and if you will join Him in the process, you will be rebuilt. That is God's promise. He wants your heart whole, and there is a very good reason for that.

Let's travel together back in time to 538 B.C. If your eyes are crossing because you think the Old Testament is old news and has no relevance for us today, do yourself a favor and read the Old Testament. It will be one of the richest reads of your life. You will see the entire character of God on display in all of its glory.

Okay, back to our time travel. Our first stop is Babylon where we meet a whole nation of people who have been exiled into bondage because of sin,

sin that wounded their hearts by drawing them away from the God who had chosen them to be His own. The Israelites were in bondage to their enemies, and like those of us who are in bondage to our wounds, some were there because of their own sin and others were collateral damage from someone else's sin.

In the Book of Ezra we witness God releasing the Israelites from bondage and giving them the opportunity to return to Jerusalem. Two hundred years before, God prophesied this moment in time through the words of the prophet Jeremiah. God wanted them to be free, just as He wants you to be free, and so Ezra 1:1 tells us that "the Lord moved the heart of Cyrus king of Persia" to release any Jews whose hearts God had moved to go back to Jerusalem to rebuild.

Ezra 1:6-7 says that all their neighbors gave them silver and gold, livestock and expensive gifts and that the king gave back all of the temple articles that had been stolen when the Israelites were taken into bondage.

Do you see what God did? Before one Jew ever started the journey out of bondage, God worked on their behalf to provide for them. *If God is calling you to come out of the bondage of your wounds, you can be confident that He is already working to provide everything you will need, as well.* All you have to do is allow Him to show you His provision.

Your need may be words of truth spoken in love (Ephesians 4:15). He has already picked the person who will speak them to you.

If you will need comfort, there is someone who has experienced the reality of 2 Corinthians 1:3-4, "Praise be to the God and Father of our Lord Jesus Christ, the Father of compassion and the God of all comfort, who comforts us in all of our troubles, so that we can comfort those in any trouble with the comfort we ourselves have received from God." That person has already been comforted by God and is waiting to comfort you when you need it.

Your need might be someone to hold your hand and walk with you on your journey to wholeness, someone who has walked this path before you and knows how difficult it can be; someone who has learned that holding on to God and trusting Him no matter how difficult the journey becomes is worth the character and faith gained and the hope realized (1 Peter 1:3-7). God has already picked the person for you and will move in that person's heart at the proper time.

It could be that you will need resources like books, tapes, or DVDs. Believe me when I say that God will place those resources in your hands, probably in some awesome, supernatural way.

There is something very pertinent to us in this account of the Israelites. Even when many of the Jewish people began to leave the place where they were being held in captivity, some chose to stay rather than go home where they belonged. Only the earnest, pious Jews returned to Jerusalem.

The Jewish people had been in bondage for seventy years. Some had been born in Babylon. Their homes and lives were established in this place of exile. That is why so many were content to stay there, because they were comfortable. They were willing to forego freedom to stay in a familiar place.

Part of me can understand their reluctance to make the journey across the desert back to Jerusalem. It would be hard, dangerous, and long. And it would end, not in the beautiful city they remembered or were told about, but in a city that was full of ruins and rubble. What these Jews didn't consider was the kindness, love, and blessing that God would extend to them. They forgot God's prophecies about this time in their history and the promises He had made to those who would return. If they had remembered, they would have known that it was worth whatever sacrifices they would have to make.

The depth of their love and devotion for God was revealed in the choice each of these Israelites made. Those who loved God and wanted to be where He would bless them; those who wanted to be free to worship God in His temple are the ones who chose to courageously venture out of bondage and into freedom, trusting God to be faithful to His promises.

When we are in bondage to the pain of our wounds, it is easy for us to think the same way these Israelites did. You may know in your heart that God is telling you, "Be free!" You know because He is tugging at your heart through things you are reading, sermons you are hearing, things other people are sharing, or even your own weariness with the way you are living. Maybe you have grown comfortable with your pain, even though your heart hurts deeply and the pain is robbing you of life. It is easy to grow comfortable with the pain and its consequences. *You may not be able to imagine life without the pain, so you are prone to choose to stay in the bondage of your wounds rather than venture out into the unknown, even if the unknown offers you healing and freedom.* You may even now choose to stay in bondage. You are looking at the journey you will have to make, and you aren't sure that it is worth the sacrifice.

What will you have to give up? What kind of hardship will it bring to your life? Will it expose a part of your past that you would rather keep hidden? Will your journey out of bondage bring pain to someone that you love dearly? Could you lose all that you hold dear?

You may be like my friend who was raped and became pregnant then had an abortion. She is haunted every day by the wound that her rapist left in her heart. The pain of the rape is not nearly as intense and destructive, though, as the wound left by her choice to take the life of her unborn child. Heaped onto that pain is the secret she has kept from her husband. Her wound eats away at her heart day after day, year after year. She is terrified of how her husband will respond and of what she could lose if she makes the journey out of bondage and begins to rebuild her heart. My friend struggles every day wondering if the blessing of the freedom God offers her is really bigger than whatever she may sacrifice to have it. She is in a crisis of faith with a huge choice to make.

In John 10:10 (NASB) Jesus says, "The thief comes only to steal, and kill, and destroy; I came that they might have life, and might have it abundantly."

When we choose to stay in bondage we are giving the thief, Satan, permission to continue to kill a part of us, to steal more from us, and to keep heaping his destruction on our lives.

When we choose to risk coming out of bondage, sacrificing whatever we must to have God's freedom and healing, we are reaching out to claim the gift of abundant life. We all choose either bondage or freedom. *Bondage is often chosen by our passivity, but freedom is always a proactive choice.* On the other side of bondage God promises not only freedom but abundant life. Will you choose life? It's yours for the taking.

Reflection & Application

1. What things in your life are keeping you from being wholly devoted to God?

2. What "prosthetics" do you put on to hide the missing pieces of your heart?

3. When you consider allowing God to rebuild your broken heart, what is your greatest fear? What are the risks you will take and the sacrifices you will have to make to be free, healed, and whole?

Chapter 9

∾

Let the Journey Begin

Have you made your choice? How I pray that you have chosen freedom and the life that comes with it. You will never regret it!

God knows the fears, hindrances, and sacrifices you are facing and He is already moving His provisions into place on your behalf. So once you start your journey out of bondage, keep going until you reach the place of rebuilding.

Let's continue looking at the Jewish people and see what we can learn from their experience. Those who chose to come out of bondage and go back to Jerusalem saw God's faithfulness to them, not only in His provision before their journey started, but all along their four-month trip. I don't know about you, but I can't imagine tromping through the desert with all of its dangers for four months. These precious people must have been motivated to continue on by the expectation of God's reward at the end. What else could have kept them going?

Surely they were seeking God and placing their faith in Him for this journey. They must have been clinging to the truth that their forefathers knew and that is recorded for us in Hebrews 11:6 that "without faith it is impossible to please God, because anyone who comes to him must believe that he exists and that he rewards those who earnestly seek him."

Let this be an encouragement to you on your journey. I know that most of us would like for God to just zap us into freedom and healing and do an abracadabra over us that puts our hearts back together, but if

He did that, think about how much of His character and faithfulness we would miss seeing.

Your journey may be shorter than four months or much longer, but however long it takes and whatever the obstacles you face, keep your focus on God and His reward the whole way as you press on to the end. Let Philippians 3:12 be your strength on the journey, "I press on to take hold of that for which Christ Jesus took hold of me." *Jesus Christ took hold of you so that you can be wholly His. Don't settle for less.*

As we go back to Ezra we see the Jewish people back in Jerusalem. They're finally home! Can you imagine the emotions they must have felt? The absolute joy of leaving the place of bondage, the difficulty of the long journey back, the apprehension of going to live in a new place, and then the heartache they must have felt when they saw the destruction that awaited them in this place that was to be their new home.

What they felt is much the same as what you may feel when you choose to respond to God calling you to come out of the bondage of your wounds and trust that God's promise of healing and freedom is just over the horizon. You will feel a full range of emotions as you move toward hope—joy, relief, excitement, fear, disappointment, frustration, grief, despair, giddiness, discouragement, anger, and anticipation.

Our journey will not be easy. That is why we want to learn from the people who have gone before us from bondage into freedom. The Jewish people knew that their first mission was to rebuild the temple, but before they started the work of rebuilding they celebrated their return by building an altar and worshipping God (Ezra 3:2-3). At the altar the people made their hearts right with God so that He could bless their work on the temple.

What an example to us!

As we follow God's leading and begin to come out of bondage, asking Him to set our hearts free from the pain of our wounds and to heal our brokenness, our hearts must first be right with Him.

The Jewish people had it right, so follow their example. Ask God to show you any barriers that would keep you from receiving His blessing and courageously remove them. Bow your heart before Him in confession and repentance so that He can bless you in your rebuilding process.

Once their hearts were consecrated to the Lord, the people began to work on the temple. They knew this was the first thing they had to do and they knew why—the temple was where God dwelt among His people in the Old Testament.

I want you to understand that God didn't tell the people to go back to Jerusalem and move on or forget the past or just put it all behind them. He didn't tell them to forgive their ancestors for getting them exiled and forget how they had disobeyed God. And He didn't tell them to ignore the rubble of the ruined temple, and just watch their step. He told them to come out of bondage and rebuild.

This remnant of God's chosen people followed His instructions and started the work of rebuilding. They laid the foundation for the temple, but then they stopped. Listen to what Ezra 3:10-4:4 says:

> When the builders laid the foundation of the temple of the LORD, the priests … and the Levites … took their places to praise the LORD…With praise and thanksgiving they sang to the LORD: "He is good; his love to Israel endures forever." All the people gave a great shout of praise to the LORD, because the foundation of the house of the LORD was laid.

What a great moment! What a time to celebrate! The foundation of the temple was complete, and now it was time to rebuild the temple itself. God was blessing the faithfulness of His people. But look what happened.

> When the enemies … heard that the exiles were building a temple for the LORD, the God of Israel … they said, "Let us help you build because, like you, we seek your God and have been sacrificing to him"… But … the heads … of Israel answered, "You have no part with us in building a temple to our God. We alone will build it for the LORD" … Then the peoples around them set out to discourage the people of Judah and make them afraid to go on building. They hired counselors to work against them and frustrate their plans.

The people were so thrilled that they threw a party to celebrate. Their celebration was so loud that the surrounding nations heard them and wanted to help them rebuild. The men of Israel were wise to say no. You may be wondering why the Jews didn't let these nations help, after all it would have expedited the process, and these nations said they had been seeking the God of the Jews and sacrificing to Him. Would it be so wrong to put the extra hands to work? Yes!

These were pagan nations. They worshipped multiple gods and to them Israel's God was just one more god to worship and make sacrifices to. They didn't recognize Him as the One True God. Their hearts did not belong to the God of the Jews, and this made these nations enemies of God and of the Jewish people. Today we would call these nations "the world."

We see their true hearts and motives in their response to being told no. The real motivation of their hearts was their fear of the religious and political implications once the temple and the city of Jerusalem were rebuilt, so the surrounding nations started harassing the Jews and trying to discourage them.

Sadly, the Jewish people gave in to the pagan nations instead of clinging to the power and the promises of God. They chose to let the world discourage them, and in their discouragement the Israelites stopped building the temple. They lost heart because they didn't expect to come up against such opposition, but they should have expected it. These Jews had forgotten that from the time God chose the nation of Israel as His own, the pagan nations had been against them. They had forgotten, too, what happened when they disobeyed God.

Are you thinking, "Nice story, but what's it got to do with me?" If you are, I'm glad you asked because I've been waiting to tell you.

First, God created every person to be a temple where *He* can dwell. His desire is for all men and women to accept His gift of salvation, so that He can come and live in their hearts. If you have put your trust in Jesus Christ as your Lord and Savior then your heart is a temple of the Spirit of God. First Corinthians 3:16 asks, "Do you know that you yourselves are God's temple and that God's Spirit lives in you?"

God wants you to rebuild the ruins of your heart, His temple, for the same reason He wanted the Israelites to rebuild the temple in Jerusalem, so that He can fully dwell there.

If you have accepted Jesus, then God dwells in you, but He can't fully reign in your heart as long as your heart is filled with the ruins of a deep wound. When your heart is already full of pain and the thoughts, attitudes, and behaviors that your pain produces, you are missing the fullness of God's blessing. You may be getting *some* of His blessing, but don't you want it all?

Second, the world wants to help you rebuild the temple of your heart, just as the neighboring people wanted to help the Jews, but the world around us is ruled by Satan. And like the pagan nations of old, it hates and fears those who belong to the One True God.

Jesus tells us why in John 17:14: "I have given them your word, and the world has hated them, for they are not of the world any more than I am of the world."

The world and Satan live in fear of the power of God that is unleashed in us when the ruins of our broken hearts are rebuilt so that God's Spirit can fully empower us. In his fear "your enemy, the devil, prowls around like a roaring lion looking for someone to devour" (1 Peter 5:8).

Your enemy wants to help you for only one reason—so that he can destroy all of the rebuilding you're doing with the Lord. Your enemy wants you to be yoked to him, because when you are, you aren't fully yoked to God.

You may have already allowed the world to help you by buying into the world's self-help tools. Store shelves are filled with books, CDs, and DVDs that the world offers. Ask almost anyone and you will be told of a program or support group that can help you overcome whatever it is that's keeping you from being the best you can be.

These things look as though they can help us get over our issues, and if you have turned to the world's solutions in an effort to get over the pain of your wounded heart, you may have found some relief. But I can assure you that you have only masked your wound, because the world's solutions drive us deeper into our self-focused, self-protective mode. They don't point you to the only One who can heal your broken heart, the only One who knows how to put it back together the right way.

If you want to rebuild your heart once and for all, you have to move your focus from yourself to God and be willing to lay your heart before God and trust Him to put it back together and protect it in the process. You have to be willing to give up control and trust God to lead you through your process of rebuilding.

Your journey into freedom, healing, and wholeness isn't a psychological or emotional journey, it is a spiritual journey, and only God can take you to your destination.

This is a personal issue for you. Your process won't look like mine or your friend's or your neighbor's. God most often leads us on our journey one step at a time, so you have to be willing to wait on His timing and instructions and believe Jeremiah 31:4, "Again I will build you, and you shall be rebuilt."

If you race ahead of God or take a detour, you will lose your way! Henri Nowen in his book *Finding My Way Home* says it this way:

To wait with openness and trust is an enormously radical attitude toward life. It is choosing to hope that something is happening for us that is far beyond our own imaginings. It is giving up control over our future and letting God define our life. It is living with the conviction that God molds us in love, holds us in tenderness, and moves us away from the sources of our fear.

Our spiritual life is a life in which we wait, actively present to the moment, expecting new things that are far beyond our imagination or prediction. This indeed is a very radical stance toward life in a world preoccupied with control.

Look at the difference between what the world says and what God says:

The world tells us to be assertive. Don't let anyone run over you; put people in their place. While there is nothing wrong with standing up for what you believe is right, this is not what the world is really saying when it says be assertive. The assertiveness of the world carries the air of prideful, forceful words and actions. I bought into this years ago, and it was nothing short of disaster for those who were recipients of my assertiveness. You see, like most other angry people, I used my new assertiveness to legitimize my outbursts of anger. When my new assertiveness was married to my anger issues, it was ugly! Most of us have had an encounter with an angry, assertive person, haven't we? And it isn't pretty, is it?

It is heartbreaking to see a gentle, shy person with no self-confidence struggle to assert themselves, especially with someone who is brash, overconfident, and even angry. I have watched many times as a gentle person steps out of his (her) true self and is met with scathing words that wound them even further.

God tells us to humble ourselves and set biblical boundaries. First Peter 5:5 tells us, "Clothe yourselves with humility toward one another, because, 'God opposes the proud but gives grace to the humble.'" Psalm 25:9 encourages us, "He guides the humble in what is right and teaches them His way." And Proverbs 11:2 is so true, "When pride comes, then comes disgrace, but with humility comes wisdom."

When you humble yourself, God has the opportunity to work in your situation *and* your heart. He will give you the wisdom to know what to say, what to do, and what boundaries to set. God doesn't expect you to let others run you over, but the response of one who has the Spirit of God dwelling in her heart should be kindness, gentleness, and self-control

(Galatians 5:22-23), not puffing out your chest and proudly asserting yourself.

The world tells us to claim our rights, to go after what we deserve.

God says deny yourself and follow Him (Luke 9:23). When we do that we are rewarded with spiritual blessings, not those we can gain for ourselves.

The world says to look out for yourself, because you're number one.

In Philippians 2:3 *God says to consider others as more important than ourselves*. Does that mean we can't look out for ourselves? No, but it does mean that we look out for others, too.

The world says, "Think positively. Get rid of those negative thoughts." If we do that, the world says all will be well. This attitude seems to communicate that we can make everything work out just fine if we put positive thought into our heads. Well, I have a comment about that: If you are sitting in a burning house, I don't care how many positive thoughts you think, the house isn't going to stop burning; and if you don't get yourself and your positive thoughts out of the house, you'll be a crispy critter!

God expects us to be wise and to think on truth, see things as they really are, and act according to His Word and His ways. You and I both know that the truth of a situation isn't always positive. In fact, sometimes it's really negative. Seeing the truth of a situation set us free to deal with it. As long as we make excuses or try to paint a rosy picture of a bad situation, we will not be able to apply the wisdom of God to it.

The world tells us we can do it. We just need to take control of our situation. This gives us false hope in ourselves and our own power and abilities. It puts us at the center of attention.

God says to place your hope and the outcome in His hands. He tells you to be controlled by the Holy Spirit and work things out in the Spirit's power (Ephesians 5:18). This gives you the only real hope that you have, the hope that comes from Jesus and His plans for you.

Do you see the difference in God's ways and the world's ways? Do you see how "me" focused the world's ways are? Do you see how the world's help places everything into your hands? Do you see how the world's help can destroy any work that God wants to do, simply because it tells you to focus on yourself and not God?

If you believe that you can find healing and freedom on your own, if you believe that you can rebuild the ruins of your broken heart yourself, why haven't you already done it?

Have you tried the world's ways and found they aren't working out the way you thought they would? There is a reason for that. *God created you, and He knows you through and through. He is the only one who knows how the pieces of your broken heart fit back together.*

Please allow me to give you a wise and stern warning here: It doesn't matter if the person is a professing pagan or a professing Christian, if the way to healing and freedom that they give you is not God-centered, if it makes you think you can do it, run the other way as fast as you can. God's way is the only way that really works.

There is a third way that the temple story applies to your journey. When you decide to deal with your wounds God's way, rather than letting the world help, criticism and an effort to discourage you will come from somewhere. Count on it, because the enemy does not want you free, healed, or rebuilt.

He will see to it that at least one significant person will move in with some sort of discouraging message, and that person could be a voice from the past that plays in the CDs of your mind.

Satan will tell you lies like:
    "You'll never change."
    "You've been struggling with this for so many years, why even try to
    change things now. Just find a way to live with it."
    "They deserve your anger. You have every right to act the way you
    do and be the way you are, after what they did to you."

Satan will put doubts in your heart with questions like:
    "What makes you think you can change things now?"
    "How is this way any different from what you've tried before?"
    "God let it happen in the first place, so why do you want to trust
    Him?"
    "Do you really think God cares that you are hurting?"

The heart of man is meant to be a temple where the Spirit of the living God can dwell. The ruins and rubble of a wounded heart make it impossible for us to live in the fullness of His blessing. Because God wants us rebuilt and Satan wants us in ruins, we find ourselves at a fork in the road having to choose to either follow God on a journey to wholeness or remain in the rubble pile of our wounded hearts. When we choose to follow

God, the world becomes an instrument of criticism and discouragement in the hand of Satan.

It's easy to get caught in the confusion between God's way and the world's way, and just give up. Don't let that happen! Instead, let your journey begin as you stand firm in the wisdom of Proverbs 3:5-6, "Trust in the LORD with all your heart and lean not on your own understanding; in all your ways acknowledge him, and he will make your paths straight."

Reflection & Application

1. In what ways and in what areas of your life have you settled for less than what Jesus Christ desires for you?

2. What do you need to do to follow the example of the Jewish people in Ezra 3 to make your heart right with God so that you can rebuilt it?

3. Have you tried the world's ways to find healing and freedom? How has that worked, for you or against you? Has it made you more God-focused or more self-focused?

Chapter 10

∾

The God of Do-Overs

I'd really like to be able to take issue with the Jewish people for giving in to the opposition, for not crying out to God for the courage to go on, and for not being so determined to do the will of God that they would sacrifice life and limb to build a house for God so that He could dwell among them. I'd also like to be able to tell you with utmost integrity that I would have forged on, focused on the goal and totally oblivious to those pagan nations. Oh, how I wish I could know for sure that I would have been a hero of the faith if I had been in Jerusalem during that time.

The only honest thing I can say is that I have done exactly what the Jewish people did, not once or twice, but over and over again. I stand guilty of having given in when Satan has mounted a campaign against me.

It's hard to keep going when you're faced with obstacles that catch you off guard and set your mind spinning with all sorts of doubts and fears.

It's hard anytime it happens, but if it happens when you are flying high, like the Jews were, celebrating with great expectation and anticipation, you don't just cave, you crash.

It seems that this is what happened to the Jewish remnant—they crashed, but they didn't burn, and they didn't just sit on their rears.

They got up, dusted themselves off, and started building again, but not building the temple. They started building their own houses, while the foundation of the temple lay there waiting for the house of God to be built upon it.

God saw the opposition. He knew what had happened. He knew how hard it was for them. After all, they were only mere men. So He understood and gave them a pat on the head, right? Wrong! God was not pleased. *Yes, they were mere men, but they had a sovereign, omnipotent God who was on their side, just as you and I do.*

Our journey back in time now takes us to a two-chapter, thirty-eight verse book tucked between the two *Z* books of the Old Testament. The book is Haggai. If you're like me, you'll have to look it up in the table of contents, but that's okay, look it up and read it, please. You may not even recognize this prophet's name because we don't pay him much attention.

I've been a Christian for almost forty years and I've never heard a sermon on this book of the Bible, but when I read Haggai, I had an "ah ha" moment that changed my perspective on dealing with the ruins of my wounded heart.

God could have just written these people off. The Jewish remnant was out of bondage because God, in His loving-kindness, had set them free and they couldn't even show their gratitude by completing the temple, the place where they would worship Him. Instead they were selfishly building for themselves. God wasn't sitting idly by while the Jews went about their own business. He sent Haggai to them with a stern message.

In Haggai 1:2-4 we see the central issue.

> This is what the LORD Almighty says: "These people say, 'The time has not yet come for the LORD's house to be built.'"
> Then the word of the LORD came through the prophet, Haggai:
> "Is it a time for you yourselves to be living in your paneled houses, while this house [the temple] remains a ruin?"

By the time God sent Haggai to speak to the people, it had been fifteen years since the foundation was laid, the temple was still unfinished, and the Jewish people were feeling the toll of their disobedience, and of not honoring God with a rebuilt temple.

Those verses tell us that the people stopped building because they didn't think it was the right time to rebuild. That was nothing more than whining and complaining because of the opposition they encountered.

Here's my interpretation of what they really said: "This is too hard. These people are saying mean things to us. If this were really God's will, it wouldn't be this hard. Why is God letting the pagans be so mean to us? It's just too hard, so it can't possibly be what God wants us to do right now. This isn't the right time, so we'll do something else for God. We'll stay busy, and God will be pleased."

Did you see yourself there? Do you believe that when you are doing what God wants you to do, it won't be hard? Many people do. They believe that when we are in the center of God's will, life is wonderful—it's easy. I've fallen into that trap a time or two myself.

If you believe that doing God's will is easy, let me ask you something. When Jesus was brutally beaten, spat upon, and nailed to the cross, was He doing what God wanted Him to do? I'm sure you're nodding yes. Now, do you think it was easy for Him? Of course it wasn't! But He did it anyway "for the joy set before Him" (Hebrews 12:2). He did it for the joy of doing the Father's will and the blessing that would come to all mankind because He did.

The Jews were making excuses and God wasn't buying it. God didn't accept excuses from them, but He was still on their side, even after they let the world sidetrack them from doing His will. He is, after all, a patient, loving God, but He is also a just God.

It would be prudent for us to pay attention to the message Haggai took to the people, because when the criticism, skepticism, and discouraging words come, you and I are prone to do just what this remnant did. We're prone to stop doing what God has told us to do, even if it is the rebuilding of our own hearts. We are tempted to do something easier; and if we do, God won't accept our excuses, but neither will He give up on us.

You may have heard God calling you out of your bondage and into His healing and freedom. You may be sick of living life as you have been, controlled by the ruins of your wounded heart. You may have even faced the piles of rubble in your life and started working either the world's way or God's way to clear the rubble away and rebuild your life. You may be like the nation of Israel, you've hit the wall of criticism and discouragement, and you've decided that it's too hard, it must not be the right time, and it would be easier to just stay as you are and suffer through it. *When we begin to deal with our wounds and it gets hard and painful, we often whine and complain ourselves into quitting.*

We want to run away and work on something else just like the Jewish remnant did. We'll dig deeper into our ministry or our work. We'll find a hobby or someplace to serve that makes us feel better. We'll work at our mothering thinking that God will be satisfied if we become the world's best mom. We may work to finally get our house organized or to be the most wonderful wife or to be employee of the year. Maybe we'll turn over a new leaf and start taking care of our bodies—we'll exercise and lose weight.

What do you run to when life gets hard or painful? I'm not talking about behaviors right now; we'll get to those later. I'm talking about things that keep you busy and preoccupied, so you can avoid the real issues of your heart. We all have things that make us feel more in control, things that give us a sense of accomplishment or a feeling of contributing.

When I want to ignore the heart issues God is asking me to deal with, I can become the most ingenious person on earth at finding other things to work on that will occupy my mind and my time.

We don't need to stop doing these things, but we do need to discern what our motivation is. Are you doing them because they give you purpose and satisfaction in that moment? Or are you doing them to take your mind off of issues that God wants you to deal with? Are you doing them because it's easier than pushing through whatever the enemy is tossing your way to discourage and dishearten you? Are you distracting yourself because it's too painful to look at your wounded heart and the mess it has made of your life?

It's easy to work at rebuilding the ruins of our wounded hearts when we are seeing progress, when we are comfortable about the process, and when the enemy is leaving us alone. But as soon as it gets hard and discouraging, we want to run. We want to run away, but we don't want to be still because then we would have to think about the pain. So we'll work on some other aspect of our lives that needs tweaking.

We will work on any other area of our lives that needs changing and run from the very thing that will change every other area of our lives. When we do that we play right into Satan's hands. He loves it. He doesn't care what you are doing as long as it isn't what God wants you to do right now.

We would be wise to look at God's response to the Jews when they went off to do their own thing. He wasn't impressed or pleased. The people had abandoned what He had told them to do in order to do something of their own choosing. He wanted the people to obey Him and rebuild the temple. And because you are reading this, you can be sure that He is asking you to obey and rebuild, too. This is your moment to choose to walk out of the prison of your pain and taste God's freedom. Will you do it?

You aren't reading this by accident. You didn't pick up this book because you didn't have anything else to read. You aren't reading this because someone strong-armed you and you didn't know how to say no.

You are reading this because God put this book in your hand, and He did it because He loves you and wants to offer you healing, freedom, and wholeness right now. You have to decide what you're going to do with His offer. This is a divine appointment for you.

How did God respond when His people ran from rebuilding the temple? He sent Haggai to them and in essence asked them, "What in the world do you think you're doing? It isn't what I told you to do." God could have handled this in myriad ways, but look what He did.

In Haggai 1:5-9a the Lord approached the people with patience and gentleness, but also with firmness. He told the people:

"Give careful thought to your ways. You have planted much, but have harvested little. You eat, but never have enough. You drink, but never have your fill. You put on clothes, but are not warm. You earn wages, only to put them in a purse with holes in it …
You expected much, but see, it turned out to be little."

God wanted them to take a good look at their situation. He wanted them to realize the futility of everything they were doing. Then in 1: 9-11 He explains to them why they were working so hard and accomplishing so little.

"What you brought home I blew away. Why? … Because of my house…which remains a ruin, while each of you is busy with your own house. Therefore, because of you the heavens have withheld their dew and the earth its crops. I called a drought … on the labor of your hands."

Whoa! God's got my attention. When the people stopped working on the temple, everything else they did was futile. God saw to it that everything they did—whether they were planting or harvesting, eating or drinking, clothing themselves, or working hard—fell short of what the people needed or expected. No matter how hard they worked, nothing brought them the results, the fulfillment, or the satisfaction they hoped for.

Why? God made the work of their hands futile, because they were not obeying Him. He told them to rebuild the temple, but they were busy doing their own thing.

In Haggai 1:8 God reminds them of why they were to rebuild, "... so that I may take pleasure in it and be honored." That is exactly why you and I have to rebuild the ruins of our wounded hearts, so that God can take pleasure in it and be honored by it. God created us to bring Him glory. We're not here to do our own thing. We're here to do God's thing, and we can't bring glory to God when we are in ruins.

Matthew 6:33 tell us, "Seek first his kingdom and his righteousness, and all these things will be given to you as well." When we focus on God and obeying Him, He takes care of everything else we need—our physical needs, our emotional needs, our mental needs, our spiritual needs. He knows our real needs and, when we seek Him first, we will never lack anything we really need!

God could have rained down hellfire and brimstone on His people, but instead He simply withdrew His blessing. He let them see what we need to learn—they weren't in control of the outcome of their labors, He was; and we aren't in control either, God is.

God does the same thing with us. If you decide to run from rebuilding your heart and life, God will let you run, but He will also let all your efforts end in futility.

Does everything you're working at, everything you're accomplishing, and everything you're gaining still leave you feeling empty and unsatisfied? Are you wondering why? I can tell you. When you and I run from rebuilding, no matter what we run to do, we take our wound and its pain with us. No matter how fast or how far we run we can't outrun our brokenness or our God.

God wants you to be healed, free, and rebuilt, and He is not going to sit idly by while you go off to do something else hoping to pacify Him. He loves you way too much!

God will let you go, but you will constantly find yourself back where you started, stumbling over the ruins of your wounded heart.

Do you feel like you have been living your life in a circle—moving from one thing to another but always ending up in the same place dealing with the same old issues? I lived that way for years. I kept working to get all the areas of my life looking like I had it all together, but then something would happen and I would be right back in the mire of my anger, suspicion, fear of rejection, and feelings of failure as I stumble over my same old issues. I'm not always the sharpest knife in the drawer, so time and again I traveled that same circle, thinking that surely this time it would take me somewhere else. It didn't.

What are the issues you stumble over? Do you run from one bad relationship to another? Do you go from one accomplishment to another thinking that surely this one will make you feel like a "somebody"? Do you publically tear yourself down hoping someone will say it's not true and you'll be able to believe it? Do you hold others at arm's length with anger, sarcasm, or aloofness telling yourself that you aren't really lonely? Do you embarrass yourself with inappropriate behavior just to get attention because your heart is screaming, "Does anybody see me?" Do you find yourself time and again trying to fix someone else because you don't have the courage to let God fix you? Do you toot your own horn because you are afraid no one else will? Do you numb your pain with substances that allow you to stop feeling and forget just for a little while?

The issues you and I deal with come from our sinful responses to the pain of our wounded hearts, and we will stumble over those issues for the rest of our lives unless we work with God to rebuild the ruins of our brokenness.

Every time you leave God's path and travel in a circle, the circle expands. The larger the circle, the farther it takes you from God and His will for your life, and the more ingrained your sinful responses become. The more ingrained the sinful responses are the harder it is for you to turn back to God.

There is a reason God is so adamant for you to rebuild the ruins of your broken heart. Your heart is His temple, and every missing piece of mortar, every brick that has been torn down, is a breach that gives Satan access to continue to wound you. He will use circumstances, people, or even your own sinful responses to the pain to wound you over and over again. Remember 1 Peter 5:8: Satan is prowling around looking for someone to destroy. And when you aren't doing what God wants you doing, when your heart is full of the ruins of a festering wound, you are vulnerable to his destruction.

The enemy will use your wounds to beat you down and destroy every part of your life. God wants you healed and rebuilt because He knows that your wounds bring absolutely nothing good to your life:

They cause you to hurt, but not feel.

They fester and become more infected.

They tear you down.

They cause destructive anger.

They ruin relationships.

They cause you to reject love.

They isolate you emotionally.

They affect your health, physically and mentally.

They cause you to question your competence and decisions.

They tell you that you have no worth.

They drive you to get even.

They make you suspicious of others and keep you from trusting.

They keep you from seeing God as He really is.

They deprive you of the blessing of becoming the person God created you to be.

They snatch your joy and peace.

They rob you of life, especially the abundant life that Christ came to give, a life filled with His joy.

God told the people to give careful thought to their ways and to the loss they had suffered as a result. I believe He asks us to do the same. Have you looked at the destruction left behind in your heart by the people or circumstances that wounded you or would you rather ignore it? Do you ever stop to think about the futility and emptiness of trying to live among the ruins of your wounded heart? Are you tired of the self-inflicted wounds caused by the destructive behaviors you've adopted in an effort to dull the pain of your original wound?

The ruins of your wounds have left rubble scattered across the landscape of your life. You can stuff it, ignore it, pretend it isn't there, or even try to remove it by yourself, but the rubble of your wounds isn't going anywhere until you decide to work with God to clean it up and reconstruct your life according to His blueprint.

You were created to be God's temple, the place where He dwells; however, He cannot fully reign until you are rebuilt. This is the desire of God's heart for you—to fully heal you, to set you free, and to fill you full with His Spirit. And whether you know it or not, this is the deepest desire of your heart, as well.

God will let you run and He'll let you travel in a circle for as long as it takes you to finally decide to do what He wants you to do so that you can move forward healed and free.

If you find yourself time and time again dealing with the same junk in your life, know this: God will not let you move on and keep going until you come back and rebuild the ruins of your wounded heart. Every time you choose to veer from the path of rebuilding, God will withdraw His blessing until you back-track to the place where you left the path and start again with Him. He is the loving God of do-overs. He will always let you come back to Him and begin again.

Reflection & Application

1. What obstacles are standing in the way of your freedom, healing, and wholeness?

2. Do you believe that when something is hard, it must not be God's will or His way? Stated another way: Do you believe that when you are doing God's will life will be easy? Do you know how you came to believe that way?

3. What do you run to when life gets hard or painful? Do you keep running to those same things even when they aren't bringing the results you hope for? Why?

Chapter 11

∾

Your Redeemer Lives

I had just finished speaking when a precious woman walked up to me and said, "I can only hope that God would do the same thing for me that He has done for you." I could tell by the way she said the words that there was no hope in her heart. I tried so hard to encourage her, but every word she spoke, even the right ones, told me that she saw everyone but herself as God's favored child.

I see people like this woman all the time—people who believe God is working for everyone but them, who believe that God reveals the deep truths of His Word to everyone but them, who believe God wants to give good things to everyone but them. It breaks my heart, because I've lived there. I have lived hopelessly believing that God could do everything His Word says, but that He wouldn't do it for me.

You may have read the last chapter and said to yourself, "That's me. God isn't blessing me. My whole life is nothing more than futility." You may feel hopeless, especially when it comes to your wounded heart and the pain that is ruining your life and relationships.

Not long ago after a seminar session, a young woman asked me if it is normal for someone to cry all the time. She shared how she would be at work and just burst into tears for no apparent reason. Her boss was compassionate and understanding, but it had been going on for so long that her job was in jeopardy. She finally asked me, "Why won't God heal my heart?"

I knew exactly what she was really asking. *She wanted to know why God didn't make it all go away.* You see, she was under the same misconception as so many others, that God's healing takes away the pain, the past, the rubble and the ruins and it magically puts everything back together again the way it was meant to be.

If that's how God did things, the Jewish people would not have gone home to a ruined temple and city. God would have brought them home to a rebuilt city and temple, and they would have lived happily ever after!

God doesn't work that way. He provides all that we need to accomplish His will, but we have to do our part. Ever since Adam and Eve were put out of the Garden because of sin, God has asked you and me to trust in His provision and work by faith, following Him as He leads us to the goal.

God isn't a magician. He is a redeemer. He has been in the business of redeeming people from the wounds of sin since the beginning of time. Nothing has changed! No matter what has happened in your life, no matter how badly you have been wounded, no matter who wounded you, God is able to redeem your life and your wounded heart. And not only able but He is waiting to do that for you.

Remember God's promise in Joel 2:25 (AMP), "I will restore or replace for you the years that the locust have eaten ...." Nothing has happened in your life that wasn't sifted through God's hand. That doesn't mean that what has happened was God's perfect will. It doesn't mean that God did these things to you. It just means He allowed it. Whatever His reason, He opened His hand and allowed the hurtful circumstances to come into your life. God didn't make it happen, sin did, but God has purpose in it.

God is never oblivious to what is happening to you. He sees it all. He is not taken by surprise when you are hurt by another person or when you make a choice that wounds your own heart. He is not shocked by the evil that wounds us because we live in a sinful world.

God sees it all, so why doesn't He stop it? Why doesn't He stop you when you are about to make a horribly stupid choice? Why doesn't He make the sin of the fallen world go away?

Whether we want to admit it or not, these questions race through our minds when our hearts are hurting. We want to know, "God where were you?" If you are in that place, let me assure you that God is where He has always been.

God decided in eternity past to give us free will. Sometimes I wish He hadn't done that, but He did. God is a just God, so He can't give you and me free will and withhold it from someone else who means to harm us. Wouldn't it be wonderful if God would let us exercise our free will for good things and then withdraw it when we are about to sin? It would save us a lot of heartache, wouldn't it? But that's not the way He works.

So where is God when sin is destroying your heart and mine? He is poised and ready to intervene when we cry out to Him in our bondage and pain.

Exodus 2:23-25 says the Israelites who were living in bondage and slavery in Egypt "groaned in their slavery and cried out, and their cry for help … went up to God. God heard their groaning and he remembered his covenant … So God looked on the Israelites and was concerned about them."

Now I want you to realize that God didn't hear them and all of a sudden become concerned, and then rush into a flurry of activity to help them. No, God had been waiting for these people, His people, to get sick of being in bondage and cry out for His help. God had already been preparing for this day when they would finally ask Him to rescue them. He was already preparing Moses to bring them out of bondage.

God sees every hurtful act that wounds our hearts, and I believe that God's heart grieves over each one. I believe it takes great restraint on His part not to hurriedly intervene, but rather to wait for us to cry out to Him. God doesn't wait in order to be mean or to cause you more harm, but in order to redeem you, and in redeeming you to show you who He is, to show you that He not only can redeem your life, but pay back all that you lost.

The last thing we saw in Haggai was God's people living in the futility of doing things their way and not God's way. God could have given up on them and left them to live in futility. Here they were fresh out of bondage, and they were already disobeying the God who set them free. You'd think that just knowing the consequences of disobedience would have motivated them to obey at all costs. But they were so much like us.

We think, as they did, that we can figure it out, that if God's way doesn't seem to be working, we can surely find a better way, and that God can't possibly mean for us to tough it out when the going is hard, or the way He has us going doesn't make any sense.

We say that when the going gets tough, the tough get going, but what we mean is that when the going gets tough, the tough go about trying to figure out a solution on their own. *Human beings are notorious for giving up, many times, when God's blessing is just around the corner, barely out of sight.*

I'm so thankful we have a patient God who isn't willing to give up on us as quickly as we are willing to give up on Him. He loves us too much to give up on us. He understands our weakness as well as He understands the deepest desires of our hearts. He is able to discern our fears from rebellion and our self-preservation from stubbornness. He doesn't accept either as an excuse for disobedience, but God will strive with those of us who have even a thread of desire to love and obey Him.

That's why God will always send someone *to* you with His message *for* you. It may be what the pastor says on Sunday morning or a co-worker speaking wisdom into your life or even the words of a song you hear, but when God sees the least bit of tenderness in your heart toward Him, He always sends His truth to you.

First Corinthians 10:13 tells us that, "God is faithful; he will not let you be tempted beyond what you can bear. But when you are tempted, he will also provide a way out so that you can stand up under it." God's truth is your way out of the bondage of your wounds. It is your way out of the temptation of living in the futility of trying to let it go, move on, or get over it man's way.

When Haggai delivered God's message, the people listened and they obeyed. Haggai 1:12 says, "The whole remnant of the people obeyed the voice of the Lord their God ... And the people feared the Lord." The Amplified Bible expresses it this way, "All the remnant of the people listened and obeyed the voice of the Lord their God [not vaguely or partly, but completely], and the people [reverently] feared and [worshipfully] turned to the Lord."

That is all God needed; that's all He wanted. He wanted them to turn their hearts to Him and listen and obey completely. That is exactly what God is waiting for you to do.

When the Jewish people determined in their hearts to obey, God made some amazing promises to them. This is so hard for me to fathom. If I had been God—and aren't we glad I'm not—I would have told them that they had to rebuild my trust. I would have put them on a standard of performance, scrutinized their every move; then if they just happened to performed to my standard, I would have made some gesture of a promise for their good behavior with a harsh warning to watch their step.

God isn't like you or me. He always disciplines disobedience because He loves us, not to spite us. Hebrews 12:10-11 explains that God "disciplines us for our good, that we may share in his holiness." It goes on to say that "no discipline seems pleasant at the time, but painful. Later on, however, it produces a harvest of righteousness and peace for those who have been trained by it."

God made the work of their hands futile to train the remnant to obey Him. *God will make the work of your hands and mine futile, as well, when we disobey Him. He does that to train us to follow Him so that we will be filled with the peaceful fruit of His Son's righteousness.* Galatians 5:22-23 tells us what the fruit of the Spirit of Christ is: "But the fruit of the Spirit is love, joy, peace, patience, kindness, goodness, faithfulness, gentleness, and self-control." This is the character of Jesus Christ that God wants to discipline into our lives.

Just as God always disciplines disobedience, He also always rewards obedience. He is a God of absolutes and He doesn't change. "Jesus Christ is the same yesterday and today and forever" (Hebrews 13:8). When we seek Him and obey Him, there is blessing every single time.

What did He promise the Jewish people, and what have these promises got to do with us?

He promised them in Haggai 2:19, "From this day on I will bless you."

The moment these people heard God's message and determined in their hearts to obey Him and begin rebuilding the temple, God began blessing them. He didn't wait to see if they would be faithful to finish the job. His blessing began as soon as they decided to obey, as soon as they turned their hearts toward Him.

God makes that same promise to you and me. He wants us to rebuild what our wounds have torn down. The moment you decide you are going to work with Him to rebuild the ruins of your heart, His temple, He begins to bless you.

When you have a heart that wants to obey, God will send His message to you, and you will know that He is speaking to you, because your heartstrings will be touched. Haggai 1:14 says that God stirred up the spirit of the whole remnant. The Holy Spirit will stir your heart to show you that the message is truth, and then you will have a choice to make. Will you heed the message you've heard and obey the Lord, even if the message is hard or doesn't make sense to you immediately?

For God to bless us we must obey, not vaguely or partially, but completely, even if the message scares us to death, even if we can't see how it could possibly do any good.

God's ways are not like ours. He doesn't think like we do. Our thoughts are filtered through the grid of our sin nature and our limited knowledge. God is holy and He knows and sees all. He doesn't just see what is going on in your heart and life right now. He sees how He can take the pain and heartache and work it for your good. He sees the things that need to be removed and added to your life. God sees the character that will blossom through His process. God sees the final outcome.

In His infinite love and wisdom, He has already planned your process for freedom, healing, and rebuilding every step of the way; and all you have to do is follow Him through it.

God has made many promises to His children in His Word, but those promises are based on our obedience to His commands. Most of God's promises are "if-then" promises because it would go against His holiness to reward disobedience, unbelief, or lack of faith.

God doesn't send us messengers or messages just to hear His words spoken. He tells us in Isaiah 55:11, "So is my word that goes out from my mouth: It will not return to me empty, but will accomplish what I desire and achieve the purpose for which I sent it."

When God speaks His message to your heart, the only acceptable response is to let His word achieve in your heart the purpose for which it was sent. This means you have to obey the message God speaks to you as fully as you know how.

God hasn't changed. When we obey He still pours out His blessing.

God made another promise in Haggai 1:13, "I am with you." God was with Israel as they rebuilt the temple in Jerusalem and He is still with His people today who are rebuilding the temple of their hearts.

He isn't just present; He is actively involved with us in our journey toward wholeness. In Haggai 2:4 God told the people that because He was with them they could be strong and work.

Moses sang in Exodus 15:2, "The Lord is my strength and my song." In Nehemiah 8:10 the people are encouraged, "The joy of the Lord is your strength."

You, too, can be strong as you rebuild the ruins of your heart, because the joy of the Lord is also your strength. When you grow weary in the process, the joy of the work that you and the Lord are doing together will give you the strength to continue on.

God sent His Spirit to remain among the people so that they had no cause to fear. In the Old Testament the Spirit of God came and went; but when Christ died, rose, and returned to the Father, He sent the Holy Spirit to live in anyone who accepts His salvation by faith. What an advantage we have as New Testament believers. We have the Holy Spirit within us and His power accessible to us every moment of every day.

Moving out of bondage, into God's freedom and healing, and trusting Him as we rebuild the ruins of our hearts can be a fearful process. It takes us into the unknown, trusting God as we may never have trusted Him before. We may wonder along the way if He can really be trusted and if He will come through for us.

Three hundred and sixty five times Scripture tells us not to be afraid— and the reason? Because God is with us. God gave us that command once for each day of the year. Do you think that, just maybe, He knew we would struggle with fear? Sure He did. He knows that we humans struggle with fear, so He is always with us so that we can run to Him with our fears and allow Him to soothe them.

He is with you because He loves you with a perfect love, and 1 John 4:18 assures you that "There is no fear in love. But perfect love drives out fear."

He is with you to guide you through the process, to show you how to rebuild and where to rebuild, to tell you when to focus on one area and then another. He wants your heart put back together His way.

He is with you to protect you from those who will try to discourage you or sidetrack you.

He is with you to give you power through His Holy Spirit to stand firm against the enemy.

He is with you to comfort you when the process is hard and hurts.

He is with you when you want to give up, encouraging you to continue on.

He is with you to bring you to the end of your process fully restored, renewed, and rebuilt.

Because God is with you, you can be strong and work hard, and you can do it without fear.

There's more. God made this Jewish remnant a promise they would never see fulfilled. They didn't see it because it wouldn't come to pass until Mary and Joseph took the eight day old Jesus to the temple to present Him to the Father. I can't imagine the glory that fill the temple that day as God the Son was presented to God the Father. It gives me chill bumps to think about how the Father must have felt when this precious baby boy was lifted up before Him and consecrated to Him. I wonder if a hush came over that place as the Christ was held up before the Father who "so loved the world that he gave his one and only Son, that whoever believes in him shall not perish but have eternal life" (John 3:16).

This is the promise in Haggai 2:7-9 that God gave to the remnant: "The desired of all nations will come, and I will fill this house with glory ... The glory of this present house will be greater than the glory of the former house."

"The desired of all nations"—I love the sound of those words.

God sent "the desired of all nations" to die on the cross for the sins of the world. He sent His precious Son for you to give you forgiveness, eternal life, and abundant life. If you have believed on the name of the Lord Jesus Christ and accepted His gracious gift of salvation by faith, the "desired of all nations" has come to you. The very thought of it takes my breath away.

God was waiting for His people to rebuild the temple so that He could fill it with His glory, and He is waiting for your heart to be rebuilt so that your life can fully express the glory of His precious Son. God wants to fill you with "the desired of all nations."

Can you even fathom it—the glory of God Almighty filling you? There wouldn't be room for anything but Him and His character and His purposes for your life, would there?

I wish you would stop reading for a moment, close your eyes and picture what your life could look like with the glory of Almighty God filling you. How would it change your thinking, your behaviors, your responses, and your desires? Wouldn't your heart be set free?

He wants to fill your heart with His glory, and don't you let the enemy tell you any differently! Satan will try to convince you that this promise is meant for everyone but you. This promise is for you, too!

I love the second part of this promise. "The glory of this present house will be greater than the glory of the former house."

If you know Bible history, you know that the first temple, the one that Solomon built, was the grandest structure ever. The temple that the remnant was building wasn't anywhere near the grandeur of Solomon's Temple. Yet God told them that the glory of the new temple would be greater than Solomon's because God would fill the new temple with His glory. The glory of the temple had nothing to do with its physical grandeur and beauty. The glory of the temple and the glory of your heart and your life have everything to do with the One who dwells there and fills it. That is why you must rebuild!

It doesn't matter how battered and bruised you are from the sin that has touched your life. It doesn't matter how scarred you are from the wounds to your heart. *When you are rebuilt and the glory of God's healing and freedom fills you, your life will be beautiful, fulfilling, and satisfying beyond your imagination.* It will make the life you had before, no matter how grand you tried to make it or fake it, look like nothing, because your rebuilt life won't be anything you can accomplish on your own. It will be what you accomplish in concert with the Holy Spirit and the power only He can give. Your life will be rebuilt to reflect the image of your redeemer, Jesus Christ.

God made one more precious promise to the remnant and to you if you will work with Him to rebuild the ruins of your wounded heart.

"And in this place I will grant peace" (Haggai 2:9).

Oh my, how I love that promise!

Our heart wounds cause upheaval in our lives that bring chaos to the way we live, the way we think, the way we relate to others and most importantly to the way we relate to God. We may look all put together on the outside, but you and I know what's really going on in our hearts and our private lives.

Some of you, like me, could win an academy award for the performance of "being okay" that we've been living, maybe for years.

Look at the promise God makes to those who will work hard and courageously to rebuild their lives and let God heal their wounds—"in this place I will grant peace."

God loves you so much and He is waiting for you to cry out to Him so that He can bring the chaos of your woundedness to an end and put His peace where chaos once reigned. He wants to end the confusion that comes from trying to figure out the why-me's and the what-if's of being wounded.

God's desire is to replace the chaos, confusion, and disorder of your ruins with His peace. Does that sound unbelievable to you? Have you been living without peace for so long that you can't even imagine how it will feel? You aren't the only one. People all around you have been living for so long in the chaos of their pain that they can't fathom a life filled with the peace of God or the hope that it brings.

Romans 5:2-5 describes the hope that the love and peace of God will bring to your heart and life.

And we rejoice in the hope of the glory of God. Not only so, but we also rejoice in our sufferings because we know that suffering produces perseverance; perseverance, character; and character, hope. And hope does not disappoint us, because God has poured out his love into our hearts by the Holy Spirit, whom he has given us. (emphasis mine)

Do you see all of these promises? Do you think God is serious about His temple, your heart, being ready for Him to indwell and fill with His glory? You bet He is!

But you have to be serious, too. You have to take a good look at the way you've been living and be sick of the life you see. You have to really desire life-change and healing. *You are at a crossroad where you can choose to go on living in your wounds and your pain, trying with all your might to fill the void yourself, or you can listen to God's words to you and grab hold of His promises and make them your own.* The choice is yours. Will you stay in the ruins of your brokenness and wounds or will you allow God to redeem the mess that sin has made in your heart?

Reflection & Application

1. Have you been living with the misconception that when God heals your heart, the destroyed places of your heart will magically be put back together? Where did that misconception come from?

2. Can you look back and see times when you have given up on God when He was trying to bless you? Describe those times. Why did you give up?

3. Do you believe that the promises God made to the Jewish people are promises that He makes to you? Which ones do you struggle to believe? Are you willing to step out in faith and let God help your unbelief? What will that step of faith look like for you?

Chapter 12

ॐ

It's Time to Get to Work

We have laid a lot of ground work: Where wounds come from, the part sin plays, the destruction to your heart, how your response can deepen your wound, wounds becoming an object of your worship, the paralysis and prison of your pain, Jesus your only hope, resolving the issue of God's love for you, and your part in rebuilding the ruins of your heart.

You have seen the Jewish people and how their journey to freedom and rebuilding parallels yours. You have witnessed their discouragement and disobedience and seen God's patience, forgiveness, and promises to them and to you. Your have seen the choice God gives you to either continue living among the ruins of your wounded heart or to join Him on the journey to freedom, healing, and wholeness.

If your response to God's invitation to rebuild with Him and find life in the process is "Yes, Lord!" then it's time to give you some practical steps that will start you on this exciting journey with God.

I can almost hear you thinking, "Finally! I thought we'd never get here." We all want the how-to's, but my experience is that most of us don't make it too far in the how-to process unless we have first taken a good look at our own hearts and motives, the why's of the process, what to expect—the good and the bad along the way—and the hope we have at the end of the process.

My prayer is that all that has gone before has served to fill your heart with anticipation and determination to stay in the journey with God to the very end.

You aren't the only one who hurts or the only one who has made this journey. There are those who have gone before you who can encourage you along the way or walk the path with you. I would encourage you to pray for God to give you a friend to talk with and pray with, someone who will be kind and compassionate with you, but will also prod you along with truth spoken in love to keep you going when you want to throw in the towel.

This is a journey of faith in the power, provision, and promises of God! So as you step out in faith, let me encourage you—don't grow weary and don't let anyone discourage you. Once you decide to grab hold of God and determine to make this journey, don't loosen your grip. Hold on for dear life. Be determined to live out Hebrews 12:1-3.

> Therefore, since we are surrounded by such a great cloud of witnesses, let us throw off everything that hinders and the sin that so easily entangles, and let us run with perseverance the race marked out for us. Let us fix our eyes on Jesus, the author and perfecter of our faith, who for the joy set before him endured the cross, scorning its shame, and sat down at the right hand of the throne of God. Consider him who endured such opposition from sinful men, so that you will not grow weary and lose heart.

There is no magic formula that will heal your wounds and set you free. Your only hope is in the redeeming power of Jesus Christ. There are practical things you can do as you partner with God. I know from my own experience and the experience of others that these action points are part of God's plan for your healing and that they will set you on the path to rebuilding the ruins of your wounded heart.

Remember to begin this journey knowing it won't be easy or quick. Be willing to participate and cooperate with God in the process for as long as it takes to be completely free, healed, and rebuild. Stay alert, watching for Satan's attacks so that you can stand firm against them.

Dan Allender says in his book *The Wounded Heart*, "When we abandon pain, we lose a sense of being intact and alive." Expect this, especially if you have lived with the pain of your wounds for a long time. Your pain may be so familiar that when it starts to go you'll feel as though you're losing an essential part of yourself. If that happens, press through it.

Allender also talks about "learned helplessness" that causes us to give up before we even try, because we believe that we will fail. If you will work with God to rebuild your heart, He promises that *He* will not let you fail.

Rebuilding is a good work that God wants to do in you, and Philippians 1:6 promises that you can be confident of this, "that he who began a good work in you will carry it on to completion until the day of Christ Jesus." *God not only promises to empower you to rebuild with Him, but He has given you the power of the Holy Spirit to keep you rebuilt for the rest of your life.*

Let me suggest that you purchase a journal so that you can chronicle your journey out of bondage and into freedom and healing and document God's faithfulness along the way. Journaling will help you to express in writing your thoughts, feelings, insights, fears, and encouraging moments. Your journal will help you to guard your heart from ever returning to the bondage of your wounds, and it will be invaluable in helping you stand firm against the enemy's attacks.

So how do you begin rebuilding the ruins of your wounded heart?

Most people don't want to hear this first point, so before you give in to the urge to throw this book across the room, hear me out, please.

The first step in your rebuilding process is **repentance**. I know this is hard to hear. I know you're probably thinking, "Wait a minute. I'm the one who's wounded and hurting. Why are you telling me to repent?"

Now that you asked, let me tell you. You need to repent, because repentance lays the foundation for reclaiming your life. Remember the masks, protective measures, and survival grids we looked at earlier? All of those focus you on yourself, not on God. Remember the "scabs" and "scars"? All of those behaviors and attitudes came from focusing on yourself and trying to take care of your own heart. When you are focused on yourself and not God your pain causes you to sin against Him and others.

Repentance is turning your heart away from yourself and your sinful, self-focused behavior and turning it toward God and letting Him take care of your heart.

When you see the sin that your wound has bred in your life—whether it's anger, resentment, hate, unbelief, self-pity, fear, or a sinful lifestyle— and you repent and return to God, you are beginning your journey out of bondage.

No one makes permanent life changes until they get to the end of their rope, until they have no desire to live any longer the way they've been living. When we see any ray of hope in our lives as they are, most of us keep going the way we're going. When we are getting some perverse pleasure from our pain or our sinful responses to it, we aren't ready to change. When your anger, self-pity, control, or hatred is filling a need in your life, you will stay on the path of destruction. *As long as you believe that you can find hope in your own response to your pain, you'll go on hurting.*

But when you get so tired of living the way you've been living, that you can't stand to go on that way any longer, you will fall on your face before God, cry out to Him for help, and in repentance lay the foundation for rebuilding the ruins of your life. That's what God is waiting for, and when you repent, God's grace is released in your life so that your heart can be healed.

Repentance starts when we see that any response to our pain or the one who caused it that doesn't acknowledge God's sovereignty, love, and goodness is sin. That is hard to take in, but it is true. No matter what has happened to us, it is sinful to respond in a way that denies the character of God.

The Bible tells you that God is holy and just. He is your comforter, provider, protector, and redeemer. He is your wonderful counselor, Prince of peace, the truth, and your Savior and friend. He is the Sovereign Lord, Almighty God, and the Creator of the universe. He is the one who knit you together in your mother's womb, the one who knows your heart, and the one who planned your days. He is love. He is patient, merciful, gracious, forgiving, and the source of your hope and joy.

God is all of these and so much more. Do you see how dealing with your pain or the one who wounded you in a way that seems natural to you denies God the opportunity to show you all that He is and all that He wants to do? Do you see how not allowing God to be God in your situation is denying who He is? Do you see that when you deny who God is, you are calling Him a liar?

I feel a need to clarify something here. Not everyone deals with their wounds in a sinful way. There is no sin in feeling the deep pain and loss that a wounded heart brings. We can ask hard questions of God and not be in sin. Struggling with doubts, fears, and deep emotions before God is not sinful. Trusting God as we make this journey with Him does not mean that we are happy, happy, happy. It does not mean that we flippantly concede to God's sovereign will. If you doubt what I say, read the psalms of David. A person can be trusting God with all of his or her heart and still struggle mightily with the pain and destruction that sin has caused.

What differentiates a response as sinful or not is what we do with our emotions, doubts, fears, and loss. If we bring them all to God and struggle through it with Him, that is not sin.

My sweet friend who lost her husband to cancer has been in the struggle of her life, but every step of the way she has been snuggled into the loving arms of her heavenly Father. Her struggle has brought her closer to Him, because she has been totally honest and open with her "Abba (literal translation is daddy), Father," letting Him comfort and calm her and reveal His purposes in all of her pain and loss.

If, however, we take matters into our own hands, trying to deal with it our way, pretending that we have within ourselves the answers and provisions we need, then we are in sin, because we are trusting in ourselves and not in God. We are focused on what we can and will do and not on who God is and how He wants to work in our lives and circumstances. When we are in sin, we need to repent. So examine your heart with God, and let Him show you what responses you need to turn away from.

In *The Wounded Heart* Allender says this of repentance:

Repentance is an internal shift in our perceived source of life. It is recognizing that our self-protective means to avoiding hurt have not ushered us into real living (the reckless abandon to God that ultimately leads to a deep sense of wholeness and joy) or to purposeful, powerful relating. Repentance is the process of deeply acknowledging the supreme call to love ... The pain of past abuse does not justify unloving self-protection in the present ... Love silences explanation, penetrates excuses, and humbles the heart, preparing that heart to be captured by the gospel of grace. Ultimately, repentance is a hungry, broken return to God.

When you turn to God with a repentant heart, you will find Him waiting to show you what He sees when He looks into your heart. I remember the fear and apprehension I felt when God began to bring all the infection—anger, resentment, lack of trust, low self-esteem, unbelief—that was in my heart into focus so that I could see it. I didn't understand why He was making me look at it, and I felt at times that God had singled me out and was punishing me for being wounded.

I learned how wrong I was when I read 1 Chronicles 28:9, "For the Lord searches every heart and understands every motive behind the thoughts. If you seek him, he will be found by you."

I was comforted to know that God searches all hearts, not just mine.

The person God used to start me on my journey toward healing and freedom suggested that I write a letter to my father telling him everything I felt about him and what he did. I wasn't sure that I wanted to put my feelings in writing, but it turned out to be one of the most therapeutic, healing steps I took.

So after you have turned your heart toward God in repentance, I am suggesting that you **write a letter** to the one who wounded you. You may be cringing in unbelief, but let me assure you that this letter will only be seen by you and God, so you can be totally honest. This letter may be to another person or it may be to yourself. Write exactly what you feel about what was done to you, the parts of your heart that were stolen from you, the things you missed out on, how it has affected your present life and relationships, and how you feel about the person or circumstance that wounded you.

This is your time to get everything that is in your wounded heart out in the open so you can see exactly what you are dealing with. Don't hold anything back, and if you're having trouble connecting with what's really going on in your heart, follow the example of David in Psalm 139:23-24. David asked for God's help to connect with what was really in his heart: "Search me, O God, and know my heart; test me and know my anxious thoughts. See if there is any offensive way in me, and lead me in the way everlasting."

Anxiety may be rising in your heart because of your feelings toward God. If that is the case go ahead and write them down. God already knows what's in your heart, so you don't have to worry about what He will think or do.

Psalm 139:1-4 makes it clear that God already knows it all. "O Lord, you have searched me and you know me. You know when I sit and when I rise; you perceive my thoughts from afar. You discern my going out and my lying down; you are familiar with all my ways. Before a word is on my tongue you know it completely, O Lord."

I pray that those verses will give you peace of mind about pouring out you heart to God. He loves you and wants to hear what you have to say. He's waiting for you to be totally honest. He's the one who wants you to rebuild, and God knows that until you know what's really in your heart, you can't bring it to Him.

You may be afraid to revisit the details of what happened to you, especially if you have been trying to forget. *This is where you have to trust that going back will actually move you forward.* If you will make the journey back with the Lord, asking Him to show you only what you need to see so you can move forward with Him, then you won't dwell on the past. You will be looking to the hope and future that will be yours as you lay the past to rest by dealing with it.

Writing down what is in your heart will move you toward your pain, and doing that will help you to stop running away from your wound and make you face the damage that has been done.

This will be painful, so prepare your heart. Before you start, revisit Jeremiah 31:3-4, "I have loved you with an everlasting love; I have drawn you with loving-kindness. I will build you up again and you will be rebuilt." God has drawn you into this process because He loves you so very much.

If you are totally honest it may be overwhelmingly painful for you to see what you've been harboring in your heart. You will have to forge on through the pain. You can trust God, as David did in Psalm 32:7, to be your hiding place, to protect you, and to surround you with songs of His deliverance.

When I wrote my letter to my dad, my heart physically hurt. I actually thought I was having a heart attack at one point. When I saw the depth of the anger and bitterness in my heart, I couldn't believe God would accept or save someone with all that ugliness in her heart. The very thought that God might suddenly reject me sent me into a spiral of despair, but God in His grace reached out and pulled me back to Himself. If you reach that point, He will do the same for you.

I encourage you to write as much as you can in one sitting. This will be an intense time, but also a time when you will feel the weight of your pain lifted. Just getting it all out will be very freeing for you.

If you have to stop, guard your heart against the enemy's ploys to keep you from going back and continuing on. Satan will do everything he can to keep you from bringing all of the heartache and sin out into the open and to keep God's light of truth from you.

If you were struggling before with your own need to repent, trust me, writing this letter to your wounder will show you far more than the emotions, hurts, and pain that he or she caused in your heart. You will find stuffed deep down in your heart sinful attitudes and desires that you need to bring to the Lord in confession and repentance.

When you have poured out your heart fully on paper, read what you have written, and **grieve over your loss and pain**. Really grieve, feel the sorrow until the hardness of your heart melts away. Some of you are probably afraid if you start crying you will never stop.

That was me. It took me years to work up the courage to let myself grieve. I really thought if I ever started, I would literally cry myself to death, but my tears became instead a cleansing rain that washed away the haze that was keeping me from seeing the hope and future God had for me. I truly wish I had been courageous enough to grieve when I first poured my heart out on paper. I did shed a few tears, but I caught myself and put my defenses back up. That was an unwise thing to do because as soon as I did, the enemy moved in and convinced me that I had to get a grip and start protecting my heart again.

I had covered so much ground on my journey. The work I had done with God had set me free from the bondage of my wound, and I was released from the excruciating pain, but being afraid to grieve delayed any further progress. It was a long time before I got back to my journey. I learned that before I could rebuild my ruins, I first had to grieve over them.

Allow your heart to grieve over what was stolen from you, over everything you lost, and over any sinful responses to your wound that hurt you and those around you. Let your sorrow bring you face down before God, crying out to Him for a rebuilt heart that will bring glory Him. If the sorrow leads you down a path of blame and hardness, don't stop grieving until you move past it and your heart is tender again.

When I grieved fully, I could feel God taking my heart in His hands and binding up its brokenness. I could feel the bleeding of my wound stop. I felt as though my heavenly Father had pulled me up in His lap and wrapped His comforting arms around me. I knew that He would never let me go, and you can be certain that He will never let you go either.

This is your journey, your process; you will make it with God as He leads. But if I may, I'd like to suggest that you stop reading for a while and lay the foundation for your rebuilt temple. Be courageous to come into the presence of your loving heavenly Father and repent of any attitudes, behaviors, or responses He is asking you to turn from. Work with Him to expose in writing the ruins and rubble that are cluttering your heart. Then fall into His loving, merciful arms and grieve until there are no more tears. With total transparency and trust, open your heart to God. The emotions, shame, and maybe even despair that surface from this part of your journey will empower you to continue on.

Repenting, pouring out your heart, and grieving before God opens your heart to be filled with the hope you have in the healing power of Jesus. *Godly sorrow allows you to experience the pain of your loss, the gravity of your sinful response, and the amazing wonder of God's grace, mercy, and love.*

Reflection & Application

1. As you read the section on repentance, what attitudes, actions, or lifestyle choices did the Holy Spirit show you that you need to turn from? How have your attitudes and behaviors denied the character of God?

2. Did you write your letter? How did going back and bearing your heart open the door for you to move forward with God?

3. How I pray that you have fully grieved! If you haven't, what is keeping you from doing so? If you did grieve, can you describe any changes in your heart that are a result of grieving with God?

Chapter 13

∾

Pressing on Toward the Goal

How's your heart? Did you stop reading to lay the foundation for your rebuilt temple? If you did, I can't help wondering how you're doing. Is your heart filled with hope or is the enemy beating you up? Can you envision your life free and healed, or is Satan prowling around trying desperately to keep you in the bondage of your pain?

Whatever is going on in your heart, whether joy and hope or fear and despair, please don't give up. Keep pressing on toward the goal of freedom, healing, and wholeness. Keep your eyes focused on Jesus, the only one who can set you free and heal you; the One by whose wounds you *are* healed.

Remember, I warned you that your enemy would try to turn your focus from God and the work you're doing with Him to either your own inability to follow through with this journey or to the one who hurt you. That's why it's important for you to **face your wounder** if it's possible. I can almost hear you shouting, "Not a chance!"

I know some of what you have just dealt with may be welling back up in your heart—fear, repulsion, rekindling of anger, or the return of guilt or shame. There may be no way that you can physically or emotionally face this person. The person may be dead, as my father is, or inaccessible. You may have no way to find the person who destroyed your life. You may not yet have the emotional or spiritual strength for a face to face encounter.

Facing your wounder isn't necessary for you to be fully rebuilt, but if the person is alive and there is an appropriate way to sit down and talk with them, I encourage you to do that.

If you decide it might be helpful for you to face your wounder, make sure you go with a humble heart. Make sure that you're going only as part of your journey toward wholeness and not to punish the person or to air your nasty emotions. It is a time to share what you feel comfortable sharing about your pain and to ask questions that may help you in your process.

If you are rebuilding from the destruction of your own naïve or foolish choices, you need to literally look in the mirror, face yourself, and have a long talk about what happened. Ask yourself the same questions you would ask anyone else.

My father died years before I started my journey out of the bondage of the wounds he had inflicted on me, so obviously I couldn't sit face to face with him. I had to be creative, so I put an empty chair in front of me and prayed. I asked God to keep me from falling apart as I went through this exercise and to make it as real as possible for me. Before you have visions of some crazy lady seeing people who aren't there, let me assure you that I knew the chair was empty.

I asked my father all sorts of questions that day and tried to imagine how he might have answered them from either side of the spectrum. I let myself feel what I might have felt if he had been there and spoken healing words to me, as well as what it would have done to my heart if he had been cold and uncaring. I had to stop many times to refocus on the Lord and pull myself together.

My goal through this exercise was to remain rational and calm and to think about what any possible responses had to do with who I really am and what my life would be like going forward. I knew that at the end of this exercise, I would either see myself as a victim or an overcomer, and it would be my choice. I knew I had to choose to place my hope either in my dead father's power over my mind and emotions or in the promises of God. I knew it was my choice to either stay cloistered behind my own defense mechanisms or to run to God and trust Him to be who Psalm 144:2 says He is: "He is my loving God and my fortress, my stronghold and my deliverer, my shield, in whom I take refuge."

Knowing the choices that were before me didn't make it easy to choose rightly. I'll be honest with you—my "session" with my father didn't go well. Because I had grown up with him and knew that he had to be right even when he was wrong, I couldn't let myself believe that if he had really been sitting across from me, he would have admitted how wrong he was and offered me an apology or asked for my forgiveness. All the pain came rushing back and I felt as if I had been whisked back to my pre-journey days. I didn't know if I could start over.

I was so overwhelmed with emotion that I curled into a ball on my bed and sobbed, talking to my father through my sobs telling him that he had never been a daddy to me, that he never loved me, that he probably wished I had never been born, that I was never good enough for him, and on and on. Things were coming out of me that I thought I had dealt with in the letter I wrote. When my sobs stopped, I heard a gentle voice in my head saying, "I'm your Abba, your daddy. You are precious in my sight and I love you. I am delighted that you were born. I'm the one who created you. I accept you completely, just as you are." I savored those words and made my choice.

When I got up, I chose to believe that God is who He says He is, and that He will do what He says He will do. From that day the pain was gone for good. I was able to walk away from what happened in my childhood and continue on with God. But I still had to do the work of rebuilding to put the missing pieces of my heart back in place.

I was so excited, so free, that I falsely believed that nothing could ever set me back even one step. How wrong I was! I decided to share with my mother the healing work God had done in my heart. Without one word of accusation, with only words of how wonderful God is, I poured my heart out to my mom. I will never forget her response. She told me I was crazy, that I had the most loving father in the world. Then she asked me if I was so love starved that I had to concoct horrible stories to get other people to pay attention to me. She told me I needed professional help, and honestly, after that encounter I believed that I did. I called my sister and all I could say was, "Tell me about our childhood." We had never talked about our childhood before, but when she finished talking, I knew I wasn't crazy.

I hung up the phone and asked God, "What do I do with this?" I already knew the answer. If I wanted to stay free and be whole, I had to give it to God and let it go. I had to believe God, not my mother.

Not everyone who faces their wounder has the desired outcome. I certainly didn't, so if you have a face-to-face encounter don't expect to hear what you want to hear.

God has honored me with the privilege of mentoring a special young woman who has a very difficult relationship with her father. It isn't just the distance created by the clashes between them, but a distance that her faith in Christ has multiplied. Her father is pretty hostile toward Christianity, and it hurts her that he cannot graciously accept her faith as her choice.

This young woman has such a desire for her father to put his faith in Jesus, but until recently her attitude toward him hasn't fostered an environment where that could happen.

After several years of prompting she finally worked up the courage to call her father, confess her wrongs in the relationship, and ask his forgiveness. His response was cordial, but not restoring. That added to the pain in her heart, but her father didn't stop hurting her there.

She's getting married soon, and her father told her he wants nothing to do with the events surrounding her wedding. She believes that it is because she and her fiancé will have a Christian ceremony. What does she do with that? Where does she go to find her great worth?

Like you and I, she cannot place her hope in the response of another person. Don't ever forget that we have only one hope, and His name is Jesus.

There are those who have faced their wounder and experienced joyous outcomes, only to realize that they are still hurting deeply. These people, too, are living with the truth that healing doesn't come from another's response, though it can help. Rather it comes from God, our Healer and Redeemer. *Our healing and freedom come from trusting that in Christ alone, we find everything we need.*

Some have found that their wound was based on false information. Their courage to finally address their issues released not only themselves but the other person to move forward and restore the relationship.

I am especially proud of one young lady whose parents divorced when she was in elementary school. Her father disappeared from her life. Her mother maliciously told her that he had never wanted children and so he chose to walk away from her. All through her growing up years, she longed for her father. Before he left they had an amazing relationship, and she couldn't believe that he didn't want her, but at the same time she was terribly wounded because he didn't try to make contact. When she was a freshman in college, she couldn't stand it any longer; she had to find her father and confront him.

When she finally found him, here's what she learned. After his repeated efforts to see his little girl, her mother told him that if he really loved his daughter, he would stay away and let her have a "normal" life. In ignorance and naiveté and filled with a deep love for his little girl, he did what he thought was best for her. His entire life was one of remorse, regret, depression, and loneliness for his baby girl. This young lady's father had stay out of her life because he honestly thought it was for her best; he had no idea that he was breaking her heart. Father and daughter have both worked with God to rebuild their own lives and to restore and renew their relationship.

My own grandmother threw away her marriage, and she and my father lived with the social stigma of divorce in the 1920s because someone told her they had seen my grandfather with another woman. No one knows if it was true or not, but without even pursuing it my grandmother set his belongings on the front porch, locked the door, and refused to ever speak with him again. My father grew up with a wound caused by what very well may have been a lie. He had no way to verify the information and my father's response to his own wound, deeply wounded each one of his children.

You may know stories of relationships between friends, family members, and co-workers that were ruined by uncorroborated information. Don't let that be the case with you. If there is any chance that your heart was wounded by misinformation or a misunderstanding, have the courage to go and find out.

I'm not saying that facing your wounder will end happily. It may end very painfully, but God is able to protect your heart whatever happens; and if you aren't willing to go, you will never know how it could have turned out.

No matter what has happened in your process thus far, even if you have had a joyful, healing outcome from the letter you wrote, from grieving with the Lord, or from talking with your wounder, you have to **realize that you can never go back** and undo what was done. It is human nature to desire to erase the reality and try to snatch back what we've lost; but we can't, it is gone. You need to resolve this truth with God and release to Him all that was lost.

I have no idea what losses you have suffered. For me it was the freedom to be a child, never learning to laugh and have fun, my innocence, my ability to trust, not knowing that I was loved and lovely. Because I wasn't encouraged or allowed to be the real me, I lost myself and spent years of my adult life learning who God created me to be. I lost years of joy, happiness, and fulfillment because of my anger toward my wounder. And since love was never modeled for me as a child, I had to *learn* to show love toward others.

You and I can never go back, but we can start over today and trust God to restore and replace the years and the things that were lost in the past.

You can faithfully work through this process and make a lot of progress toward healing and freedom; however, you can never be completely healed and free or rebuilt, **until you forgive!**

Don't think that we are just getting around to the subject of forgiveness because it holds less importance. I waited until now to discuss forgiveness because it may take you this far in the process to even think about forgiving. Every step you've taken in your journey thus far should have helped prepare you to forgive the one who wounded you.

If your heart is resistant to forgiving, you need to know that forgiveness is absolutely necessary for you to move out of bondage and into healing and freedom. Unforgiveness breeds anger, which will allow a root of bitterness to grow in your heart. The Bible speaks very clearly on this subject. Hebrews 12:15 commands us to "see to it that no one misses the grace of God and that no root of bitterness grows up to cause trouble and defile many." Ephesians 4:31 tells us, "Get rid of all bitterness, rage, and anger." When your heart is filled with anger, bitterness, and unforgiveness, you are not living in the grace of God. God's grace is His undeserved favor to you. *In pure grace Jesus Christ died on the cross so that your sins could be forgiven, and there is no way that you can understand God's grace toward you when you are unwilling to forgive another person.*

Anger and bitterness are destructive beyond what we can see or imagine. They wound us and others over and over again, and they are probably the most prolific generational wounds. Angry, bitter people breed angry, bitter people.

I once heard a rabbi say that allowing anger and bitterness to grow in your heart is like taking poison and expecting the *other* person to die. I can't think of a better illustration of what happens when anger and bitterness reign in a heart.

I can testify to the truthfulness of that observation. The people whom I was trying to punish with my anger, in reality, didn't even realize the anger and bitterness I was spewing in their direction. There was so much geographic distance between us and so little communication that they had no idea of the absolute hatred in my heart toward them. I falsely believed that the distance I kept from them was making them sad and lonely for me; that they were pining away over my absence from their lives; that they were just dying to see me. What a joke! When God finally got hold of my heart and I knew I had to move toward reconciliation, what I found was that my whole family had gone on with their lives as though I didn't exist.

While they went on with their lives, I was stuck in the prison of my pain and being eaten alive by my anger and bitterness. The only people who suffered as much as I did were my husband and children and a few innocent bystanders who received the brunt of my anger. *We think that we are hurting the other person back, but the very weapon we try to use against them gets turned on us—sucking out our very life.*

So you must forgive because it is in forgiving that you release the anger and begin digging out the root of bitterness in your heart.

You may be struggling with forgiving your wounder because of the many misconceptions about forgiveness, so let's take a moment and clear up most of them.

1. Forgiveness doesn't mean that you are condoning the behavior that wounded you, and it doesn't let your wounder off the hook. God will hold your wounder responsible for his or her actions. No one gets away with sin. Everyone suffers the consequences of their own sin. You can trust God to deal justly with your wounder, so leave it in His hands.

2. Forgiveness doesn't mean that a relationship will be restored. So often when we grant forgiveness to another, we expect them to say they are sorry, to acknowledge how bad they have been, or to feel grateful for the grace we have shown them.

In an effort to restore a relationship we often give the other person an opportunity to repent by saying something like, "You really hurt me, but I want you to know I forgive you." Our hope is that the other person will show remorse, but that may never happen. The other person may not be willing or even care to restore the relationship. They may never understand the pain they have caused.

3. Your granting of forgiveness is not contingent upon the other person's response. God commands us in the Bible to forgive, but He never makes us any promises about how the other person will respond to that kindness.

In Matthew 6:9-13 we find the Lord's Prayer. Most people can recite it by heart, but many just skim over the words in verse 12 that say, "Forgive us our debts as we also have forgiven our debtors." Think about that. If you pray that prayer, you are saying to God, "Forgive me as I forgive." Well, what if you don't forgive? Do you really want God to forego forgiving you?

In verse 15 Jesus said, "But if you do not forgive men their sins, your Father will not forgive your sins." That's pretty powerful, don't you think?

Ephesians 4:32 instructs us to "be kind and compassionate to one another, forgiving each other, just as in Christ God forgave you."

Matthew 5:44 challenges our human sensibilities saying, "Love your enemies and pray for those who persecute you." That really makes no sense to us, does it? No, it doesn't, until we realize that Jesus forgave Judas for betraying Him, and He forgave the men who brutally beat Him, demeaned

Him, and nailed Him to the cross. He even forgave His chosen people, the Jews, for rejecting Him, their promised Messiah.

Jesus knows what it is like to forgive those who don't deserve it! After all He forgives you and me. He knows what it is like to forgive those who don't show remorse. He knows what it is like to grant forgiveness and not have the other person respond in a way that offers healing.

4. Forgiveness is a choice. It is choosing that you will no longer hold the offense against the one who wounded you, whether it is another person, yourself, or even God. It is laying aside the hurt with the intention of never picking it up or bringing it up again. The choice you make about forgiving will determine whether you will be a victim or an overcomer.

5. My experience is that forgiveness is usually not a one-time-and-it's-over-and-done-with decision. I found myself having to confess, "Lord, I forgave and now I've taken it back. Forgive me. I forgive once again, and with your help it will stick this time." It took me several years of forgiving over and over again before finally one day I realized I had forgiven for the final time and it was a done deal in my heart.

6. Forgiveness is not an instant cure. I once heard a pastor tell the story of his father's death. He shared about the intense anger he had toward his dad. He told the congregation that at the funeral he stood over his father's grave, spewed all of his anger, forgave his father, and then he moved on. He looked out at the people and made this statement, "I forgave and moved on and you need to do the same." The way he said those words made me question if he had really forgiven his father from the heart. Though I cannot judge that situation, I do know this—forgiveness is not the end of your process. Often it is just the beginning. *Forgiveness is absolutely necessary, because it sets you on God's path to move forward in your process of rebuilding.*

7. Forgiveness sets you free and releases the other person, but it does not rebuild the ruins of your life. Just because you forgive does not mean the past will magically vanish and all things will be made right. It doesn't mean that you will suddenly regain all that was stolen from you or that the missing pieces of your heart will fly in from the great beyond and fall perfectly into place.

You still have to work with God to put what was stolen or lost back into place God's way. Forgiveness opens your heart to receive back from God all that you lost and be restored to Him, but you will never move on until you trust Him to heal and rebuild your heart.

8. Forgiveness doesn't mean that you will forget. I was told many times to forgive and forget, but because I couldn't forget, I thought I couldn't

forgive either. I don't believe that God tells us to forget. In fact I know He doesn't, because He often cautions me to remember where I have come from. If God meant for us to forget as a condition of forgiving, we would never be able to tell our story. I wouldn't be able to share the truth of God's healing and freedom with you. We are commanded to forgive, but I haven't found in Scripture where we are commanded to forget.

People tried to persuade me with Psalm 103:12, which says that God casts our sins as far as the east is from the west. As I prayed over that verse and studied it, I realized that the east and west are so far from each other that they will never meet in a way that points an accusing finger at you or me. Jeremiah 31:34 says, "For I forgive their wickedness and remember their sins no more."

People also quoted that verse to me. Again I will say that as I prayed about that verse, I believe God taught me that it isn't that He forgets, but rather that He will not hold a forgiven sin against the sinner or condemn him or her because of it.

God commands us to forgive, but to forget would rob us of the opportunity to tell of His faithfulness. What would we say to others if we had to forget in order to forgive? "God was so faithful to empower me to forgive. I can't remember what I forgave, but it was something bad. God was so faithful to heal me, but I don't know from what. I can't remember how, but I know He was faithful." How ridiculous would that be?

God wants you to do the same thing He does. He wants you to hold the offense that wounded you so far away that you will never again use it to point an accusing finger at the one who wounded you. The only way you will ever hold an offense that far from your heart is to place it in God's hands. *The only way you will be able to place the offense in the hands of God is by the power of the Holy Spirit that comes to live in you when you put your life into Jesus' hands.*

Rebuilding is hard work. It takes us out of our comfort zone and into some risky places. From time to time we may stumble over a pile of ruins that has yet to be removed. We may get confused by God's blueprint and wonder if we've been given the right plans for rebuilding our hearts. We will shed more than a few tears as we push ourselves to work far beyond our own limits, and learn to work, not in our own power, but in the power of the Holy Spirit.

No matter how hard your process is, no matter how long the journey takes, it will be worth any discomfort, pain, or tears to have the beauty and blessing of a heart rebuilt by God's design, restored by His grace, and renewed by His love and faithfulness.

Reflection & Application

1. Did you face your wounder in person or in your imagination? What did you learn? What benefit and rebuilding came to your heart through that encounter?

2. Have you let go of the things that were lost? If you are having trouble letting go, can you articulate why? It may help you to write down what you believe you would gain by having back what was lost. Will you trust God to give those things back to you with His replacements?

3. Where are you in the process of forgiveness? What holds you back from releasing your wounder to God? How has your unforgiveness hurt you and others?

Chapter 14

∾

A Sword? You've Got to be Kidding!

Are you beginning to glimpse a life lived in the freedom and healing of God's mercy and grace? Have you stepped toward God in faith and begun to lay the foundation for putting the pieces of your heart back together? Or are you still standing in the shadows afraid that the life you envision is out of your reach?

God makes you a promise in Psalm 147:3 that "he heals the broken hearted and binds up their wounds." You need not be afraid that God will let you down or that you will fail if you make this journey with Him.

God has given you everything you need for the journey. He has given you the only tool you will need to clear away the rubble of your broken heart and put the ruins back together so that you are restored, renewed, and rebuilt.

God has given you, not a hammer and nails, but a sword. You may think that a sword is an odd tool for building, but this is no ordinary sword. God has given you the Sword of the Spirit, His Word, the Holy Scriptures found in the Bible. In the Bible you will find everything you need for your journey out of bondage and for your rebuilding process.

So get into God's Word and let God's Word get into you. It is a soothing balm that will heal your wounds. It is your source of courage, peace, joy, and hope.

As you read your Bible and see God's unfailing love for you and the promises He has made to you, your heart will be overwhelmed with joy. Lamentations 3:22-23 promises that "Because of the Lord's great love we are not consumed, for his compassions never fail. They are new every morning; great is your faithfulness."

Your heart will never be completely healed and rebuilt without the Word of God, without His great love toward you, and without His compassion and faithfulness given to you new every day.

The Word of God will build your faith to trust Him throughout your journey of healing and rebuilding.

Romans 10:17 says, "Faith comes from hearing the message, and the message is heard through the word of Christ." The message of God's Word is far more than the gospel of salvation. It is the message of a faithful, loving God who provides for every need His children have and guides them through every step of life.

The more you are in God's Word, the more you choose to believe His promises, the more your faith in the faithfulness and love of God will grow, and the more you will know that you can trust Him to take you through this process and bring you to the end of it fully healed and whole.

There will be times when you struggle with believing that God's Word is true and that it is true for you. When those times come, you need to tell God of your struggle to believe. You can exclaim like the man in Mark 9:24, "I do believe; help me overcome my unbelief!"

I never realized the power of that verse until my almost rebuilt heart was shattered once again. It was during this hard time that God taught me most of the truths I've been sharing with you.

Some years ago my precious, stubborn, self-sufficient daughter walked away from God and decided to try life on her own. Before she came to her senses she had a drug problem and a precious little boy born out of wedlock. During the three years of her rebellion my heart felt like she had ripped it out of my chest and stomped it on the ground. I wanted so desperately to believe that God was going to intervene and make things all better, but I was having a hard time believing because the more I prayed the more distant my daughter seemed. I would write God's promises on 3x5 cards and carry them with me and I would tell God this: "Lord, I know the verse on this card is your Word, and I want to believe it but I don't. I refuse to give up on my daughter and You are the only hope I have, so I will say these promises out loud until you make my heart believe them and make them come true in her life." I was in essence saying, "Lord, I believe. Help me overcome my unbelief." God helped me overcome my unbelief! He wrote those verses on my heart, and he made them true in my daughter's life. Every time I read out loud the verses I had written on those cards, I was hearing the Word of God. Faith comes from hearing the Word of God and I saw my faith grow by leaps and bounds as God worked in my heart and also my daughter's.

The only way the ruins of your heart will be rebuilt God's way is if your heart is rebuilt with truth. John 17:17 tells us what truth is. Jesus says to God the Father, "Your word is truth." God's Word is the only place where you will find absolute truth about yourself and your situation. The words of God found in the Bible are the only ones that will silence the destructive voices from your past, the lies of the enemy in the present, and the hurtful attacks of people around you. You can tell yourself many different things trying to undo the damage done to the way you see yourself, others, and God, but only truth will permanently replace the destructive messages. God's Word is truth.

Over time God's Word will replace the destructive tapes that the enemy plays in your mind. You can't just stop thinking destructive thoughts and lies; they must be replaced by truth. If you don't replace the destructive lies with something true, there will be a void left for Satan to fill with more lies as he seeks to destroy all the rebuilding that God wants to do in your heart.

The Word of God truly is the only way you will make the journey out of bondage and into freedom. God's words are the only guaranteed building materials that broken people have.

God's words are the bricks you will use to rebuild the broken down places of your heart. Your faith placed in God's truth is the mortar that will hold the bricks in the wall of your heart.

God's Word is your roadmap out of bondage. According to Psalm 119:105, God's Word is a lamp to your feet and a light to your path. It not only shows you where you are in your journey, but where you are going with Him. It is also your blueprint for rebuilding, so pray as the psalmist did in Psalm 86:11, "Teach me your way, O Lord, and I will walk in your truth."

Rebuilding the ruins of your wounded heart is a transformation process that takes your heart from being a broken-down pile of rubble to being the place where the fullness of the living God can dwell.

Romans 12:2 tells us, "Be transformed by the renewing of your mind. Then you will be able to test and approve what God's will is—his good, pleasing and perfect will." God's good and pleasing and perfect will is for you to be filled full with His glory—His splendor, majesty, perfection, honor, and radiance displayed through His divine attributes.

You cannot be free, healed, and full of God without His Word. Only God's Word can transform your heart, and for you to be rebuilt your heart must be transformed.

Hebrews 4:12 says, "For the word of God is living and active. Sharper than any double-edged sword, it penetrates even to dividing soul and spirit, joints and marrow; it judges the thoughts and attitudes of the heart."

The Word of God never grows old. It wasn't just for the people in Bible times. It is for people of every generation. It is living, so it is always appropriate for the cultural and personal issues of the day. Sin and mans' needs may evolve over time and take on a different look, but they are the same as they have always been, and God's Word still has the answers we need.

The Word of God is forever active and so it will penetrate your innermost being and allow you to see the parts of your heart that God needs to transform in order to rebuild your brokenness.

Your heart will only be transformed as your mind is renewed to think the way God does. You are transformed when you begin to see things God's way and respond to them the way His Word tells you to respond. Proverbs 23:7 tells you that as you think within yourself, that is who you are, so if you want to be the person that God says you are, then you have to believe the truth so it can change the way you think and bring transformation to your heart.

Your heart can't be transformed as long as the pain of your wounds has a stronghold in your heart. A spiritual stronghold is exactly what it says: It is something that has a strong hold on you. It can be an attitude, an emotion, a thought pattern, or a behavior.

Second Corinthians 10:3-5 teaches us:

For though we live in the world, we do not wage war as the world does. The weapons we fight with are not the weapons of the world. On the contrary, they have divine power to demolish strongholds. We demolish arguments and every pretension that sets itself up against the knowledge of God, and we take captive every thought to make it obedient to Christ.

We don't fight as the world fights, seeking our own advantage and selfish desires, and we don't use the same weapons. Our weapon is the Sword of the Spirit, God's Word, not hateful words, manipulative behavior, or power plays. That is why responding to your woundedness with anger, self-pity, bitterness, hatred, feelings of worthlessness, unbelief, fear, resentment, guilt, shame or some destructive lifestyle will never bring you what you are looking for. The world's ways of getting even with vengeful anger or hateful behavior will not bring you the feeling of satisfaction or power over the other person that you seek. Self-pity or self-abasement will not bring the caring attention that you hope for. Living with guilt and shame, constantly beating yourself up, will not cause you to be a better person. Living in fear will not protect you from more harm, and the vigilance it promotes will only steal your peace of mind. Trying to prove your worth through accomplishments or material gain will not satisfy your need to know how precious and special you are.

When we fight the way the world does, using the world's weapons, we will always need more and more of whatever we're doing to satisfy our needs and longings. Destructive thoughts, words, or behaviors will never fill the void that our wounds have left.

Every weapon the world uses is seeking an outcome that only God can give. The weapons of the world argue with truth and cause us to live a life of pretense that keeps us from knowing God intimately.

The only way that you will break down the strongholds that your wounds have built in your heart is to use the power of the Holy Spirit to take your destructive thoughts captive to Jesus Christ and replace them with the Word of God.

When your own thoughts or someone else's words tell you that you are worthless and stupid, remind yourself of what God says to you in Isaiah 43:4, "You are precious and honored in my sight and ... I love you."

When you feel weak and unable to go on, when you think that you can't take any more, remember 2 Corinthians 12:9, "My grace is sufficient for you, for my power is made perfect in weakness."

When you feel as though you have lost your way and you don't know which way to turn or what to do, cling to the words of Isaiah 30:19, 21, "How gracious he will be when you cry for help! As soon as he hears, he will answer you. Whether you turn to the right or to the left, your ears will hear a voice behind you saying, 'This is the way; walk in it.'"

God's Word is your weapon against every hurtful and destructive thought, attitude, emotion, or behavior that comes from the pain of your wounded heart.

Remember Galatians 5:1, "It is for freedom that Christ has set us free. Stand firm, then, and do not let yourselves be burdened again by a yoke of slavery." How will you stand firm? How will you protect yourself from the attacks of the enemy so that you are able to stand firm?

Ephesians 6:17 tells you that the Word of God is the sword of the Spirit that will protect you as you stand firm against the enemy's attacks. His Word will give you the strength and courage to stay in the process.

God's Word is the only weapon you have that will defeat the enemy who wants to keep you in pain and destroy you. In God's Word alone you will find life and healing for your wounded heart. Deuteronomy 32:47 says this of the words of God, "They are not just idle words for you—they are your life."

If you desire to be free from the prison of your pain, to have your heart completely healed and whole, and to be filled with God and His glory, then you must ask God to help you believe that His words are the words of life. Ask God to help you believe that the way He tells you to live, to treat others, to respond to wrongs done to you, and the way He tells you to relate to Him are the only ways that will bring you the life, fulfillment, and satisfaction that your heart desires. *God's words give life that satisfies the deepest longings of the human soul.*

In the appendix are scripture references which will help you find verses that hopefully will speak to your specific struggle. I encourage you to get into God's Word and find those verses. Read the Bible for yourself every day, and as you do, ask God to meet with you and teach you. The Holy Spirit will speak to you through the words you are reading and cause verses to jump off the page and catch your attention. Through those verses He will give you answers and solutions for whatever is going on in your life, your mind, and your heart.

Look at your pain and the things you have lost, and find verses you can claim for your own healing process, Scriptures that will show you the truth about God, the truth about your wound, the truth about you, and the truth about your life.

You will find in Scripture words of comfort, courage, and exhortation. You will find God's precious promises to you. You will see the way He wants to work for you and in you. God's Word will change the way you think, not necessarily about your wound, but about your wounder, about yourself, and about God and who He is in the midst of your suffering.

When the Holy Spirit guides you to verses that are especially meaningful, memorize those verses so that He can bring them back to your remembrance at a later time when you need them once again. That is part of the Holy Spirit's job according to John 16:13. He is called the Spirit of truth because He is the one who guides us into the truth we need when we need it and helps us to understand it. John 14:26 says that the Holy Spirit teaches us all things and then reminds us of them later. See, God hasn't left you on your own. He has given you a helper, but the Spirit can't remind you of what you don't know. You have to be in God's Word so that He can bring to your mind the encouraging, comforting, and even admonishing words you need at just the right time.

When you find words from God that touch you in the most tender parts of your heart or you read truths that you are having trouble believing, pray those words of Scripture to Him. First John 5:14-15 tells you, "This is the confidence we have in approaching God: that if we ask anything according to his will, he hears us. And if we know that he hears us—whatever we ask—we know that we have what we asked of him."

I just love that promise and I claim it often. I'll give you an example as it pertains to wounds. My mother was very hard to get along with. Often when I was visiting she would say hurtful things to me that could have wounded me deeply if I had let them, and not only that, they could have caused me to lash out at her in impatience and anger. My mother was very hard to love. When I was with her, I had to pray more fervently than usual for the Holy Spirit to give me the power to live out the fruit of the Spirit. If I hadn't known what the Scriptures say those qualities are so the Spirit could bring them to my remembrance, I would have been in a "world of hurt." Without those words of Scripture and the power of the Holy Spirit to help me to have those qualities when I was with my mother, my responses wouldn't have been pretty.

There are other times I identify with the psalms David wrote when his heart was distressed and doubting. Over and over again we see him pouring out his heart, wondering if God was really listening to him and working on his behalf. One of those is Psalm 102. Because I can't always see progress in my journey, because there are times when I feel that God has forgotten me, and because it is so easy to get discouraged to the point of giving up, I will pray these psalms of David to the Lord. They express what I am feeling when I can't seem to put it into words for myself. The psalms always bring my focus back to God and who He really is.

At other times my heart is so overwhelmed with gratitude and praise that I can hardly speak! In those times I often use the words of one of the writers of Scripture to express my heart. There are wonderful psalms of praise, as well, that help me put my praise and gratitude into words.

Any time I want to be absolutely sure that I am praying according to God's will, I pray Scripture. Any time I can't find my own words, I pray Scripture. You can do that, too. You can let the words of the Bible express your heart for you, but to do that you have to be encountering God through His words to you, so that you know for yourself what those words are and where they are in the Scriptures.

As you begin to grab hold of specific truths and words that God gives you, you will find the pieces of your heart being put back together. You will realize that God is giving back to you everything that you lost and everything you need to make your heart whole.

Because I am committed to spending time in the Scriptures daily, I have seen that, without a doubt, God can give me back the things that were stolen from me. He has given me confidence, not in myself but in Him. He has taught me how to trust. He has taught me that with Him I will succeed, but when I fail there is forgiveness and another chance to get it right. One piece at a time God has made my heart whole as I have done my part in rebuilding. One piece at a time He will make your heart whole, too.

God's Word is the glue that will hold each piece of your heart in place until it is put completely back together God's way.

As you get into God's Word every day, looking for God and listening to what He is saying to you, His words will get into you. You will see God more clearly and know Him more intimately. You will find that your love for Him is growing deeper by the day. The more you see Him as He truly is and the more you grow to love Him, the easier it will be for you to trust Him with your heart.

The more you trust Him, the more you will obey Him, but not out of fear or compulsion. It will be because you truly want to obey this phenomenal God who loves you. The more you obey and receive the blessing that accompanies obedience, the more you will seek Him; and the more you seek Him, the more of Him you will find. This is the cycle of blessing that is yours if you will set your heart to seek God in His written Word.

Keep your Sword handy. Learn to use it well. It is the only tool you have to rebuild the ruins of your wounded heart.

Reflection & Application

1. What place does God's Word hold in your life? Answer honestly. Is it a priority?

2. Do you believe that God's Word has the answers to all the issues you face from your wounds? Do you believe it is absolute truth and your absolute authority?

3. Is your knowledge and concept of God based on your personal knowledge of the Scriptures or on what someone else has told you? Will you spend time in God's Word daily getting to know Him? What has kept you from spending time in the Scriptures in the past, and what will keep you from doing that now?

Chapter 15

༺

Embrace Your Story

Your journey of rebuilding has many stops along the way. For God's grace to be released in your life, you must stop first at the place of repentance. Repentance sets the course for the rest of your journey out of bondage. Your next destination will expose your deepest pain, your most destructive responses, and the losses that have stolen parts of your heart. If you honestly pour out your heart on paper you will connect, maybe for the first time, with yourself.

Until I wrote my letter, I had no idea how out-of-touch I was with my own feelings or my true needs, wants, and desires. I would have to say that for most of my life I was numb. Because I lived for so many years afraid to connect with my own heart, I found that I really didn't know what was going on there.

Maybe you can relate. I used to cringe when someone asked me how I felt about something that happen to me or about words that were spoken to me. I most always replied, "I don't know."

I had a friend who just irritated me to death because she wouldn't settle for that answer. She would probe with questions that I either couldn't or didn't want to answer. She seemed determined to make me connect emotionally with myself, something that I wasn't ready to do at the time. Bless her heart, she never gave up even when I retreated to my safe place—anger.

Before I wrote my letter, I really thought that anger was what I felt most of the time, but as I honestly tried to connect with my emotions, I saw that anger was a wall I hid behind so I wouldn't have to face what I was really feeling.

Grieving with God was one of the most difficult things I have done in my life. When I first read what I had written, it made me angry! I saw the emotions and losses I had put on paper as weakness in myself. My whole life I had prided myself in being a survivor. Acknowledging all the other thoughts and emotions that were going on in my heart made me feel like a wimp. It was so difficult for me to face the reality that I had indeed survived my childhood, but I had not lived it.

By the time I came to the end of my grief, something very freeing had happened—for the first time in my life I had embraced my real story. I know that may sound weird to you, and you may be wondering how a person can *not* embrace their story. After all it is what it is, right? Yes, a person's story is what it is, but that doesn't mean that we see things as they really are.

Until I poured out my heart and grieved, I had never been able to examine my life and, without shame and guilt, accept every part of my story. I had spent my life telling myself it wasn't that bad, that my parents had done the best they knew how, that I had it a lot better than many others, and that it hadn't really affected who I was.

I had even at times tried to convince myself that my childhood was pretty good; and when I couldn't come up with anything else, I told myself it was somehow my fault, not my parents'. I felt that if I had just been a better child maybe they wouldn't have done some of the things they did. I think doing that relieved some of the heartache of what I had missed and who I had become. It helped to blame myself; I knew I would never change my parents, but I could change me.

When I shared my story, it was always a matter-of-fact account. I most always began with "my father" or "my parents" or "the home I grew up in." Rarely did I begin with "I." I didn't want to make my story personal to me. I was far more comfortable holding it at arm's length making it about others.

Too often in our pain we want to reject our real story and write another one that is more pleasant. I didn't want to be the little girl who was unloved and unappreciated. I didn't want to admit that I was diminished every time my mother or my siblings made fun of me. I felt like the odd man out when it came to talents and interests. It was too painful for me to admit that my sense of worth was stolen every time I was told that I was stupid or that I would never amount to anything. I didn't want to go through the anguish of trying to figure out what was so wrong with me that a grown man would justify inflicting such physical pain on a small child.

I was uncomfortable thinking about and telling the "I" part of my story, so instead I made it about "them." My father was mean and uncaring. My siblings ganged up on me. My mother was afraid to protect her children. My father was a bully. My mother was weak. My siblings made fun of me because they didn't understand me. No one appreciated the boldness and intensity of my personality, just because they were afraid to stand up to our father and I wasn't. My father was this; my mother was that; my siblings were the other because I didn't want to face who *I* was because of my wounded heart.

When we make our experience about the other person, we don't have to face ourselves, our pain, or our shortcomings. Making it about our wounder lets us tell ourselves that we aren't really that wounded or that we aren't damaged goods, but we are.

Until we fully embrace our real story, the "I" part of our story, we will live as someone we're not, and we will miss the fulfillment of our greatest need—to be known and loved.

Until you embrace your real story and all the damage and heartache that go with it, you can't lay it at the feet of Jesus and see Him redeem it. Remember how God waited for the Israelites to cry out to Him before He stepped into their situation? He waits for you, too. God redeems what we bring to Him, so face your "I" story and watch in awe as He redeems it.

Until you embrace your real story completely you will miss opportunities to step into the lives of others and offer them hope that you know in your heart to be life-changing. You may offer others hope, but it will not be hope that comes from your own experience. You and I both know the impact on our hearts when we see God's transforming work in someone else's life. No one can argue with or deny the reality of a person's God-story. So embrace your entire story—the "I" part and the "them" part—so that He can give you a God-story to share with others who need to hear it.

Until you embrace your story in light of God's sovereignty, you won't rebuild your broken heart completely because you won't be able to see the full extent of the damage of your wound or experience fully the grace and mercy of God.

Until we allow God's mercy and grace to redeem the bondage and brokenness of our wounds, until we admit to ourselves who we have become in our woundedness, we are apt to throw stones from the rubble pile of our broken hearts as we desperately try to prove and protect the person we would rather be.

Genesis 50:20 says that what man means for evil, God intends for good and uses for His purposes. God wants to bring good from your pain, but how does that happen?

It happens as we turn to God, crying out to Him to do something for us that we cannot do for ourselves. It happens when we stop trying to deal with our woundedness our way and admit that nothing we can do will accomplish the outcome we desire.

God brings good from what man meant for evil when we lay whatever happened in our past at the foot of the cross, accepting the death of Jesus Christ as payment for our sins and His resurrection as our guarantee of eternal life.

God brings good from our pain when we place our future in the hope that only comes from Jesus Christ and His promise of abundant life now and eternity with Him.

God brings good from all of the bad when we trust Him enough to begin living James 1:2-4: "Consider it pure joy, my brothers, whenever you face trials of many kinds, because you know that the testing of your faith develops perseverance. Perseverance must finish its work so that you may be mature and complete, not lacking anything."

Experiencing joy in the trials we face because of our wounds comes from our willingness to give thanks to God, even in our pain. Ephesians 5:20 instructs us to always give thanks to God the Father for everything, in the name of the Lord Jesus Christ.

First Thessalonians 5:18 tells us to "give thanks in all circumstances, for this is God's will for you in Christ Jesus."

It makes no sense at all to be thankful for the bad in our lives until we realize that often God allows us to suffer trials so that we will turn to Him. He knows that anything that causes us to turn our hearts and minds to the sovereign Lord of the universe can only bring good to our lives. We were created by Him to live in relationship with Him, but few of us turn to God when life is good. Our faith and hope in God grow when we turn to Him in the hard things of life and we see His character and faithfulness working on our behalf.

We must not forget that the perseverance, character, and hope that are built into our lives through suffering do not come to us when life is as we think it should be. All of these things come as we see God take what man meant for evil and turn it around for our good.

As hard as it is for us to believe, there is a purpose for our pain. God can and will use all the bad from our wounds for good in our lives. What does that look like in real life?

Let's go back to some of the stories from chapter 2:

The young wife whose husband's addiction to pornography brought betrayal and despair to her heart decided to entrust her husband and her marriage to God and give Him the chance to change her husband and her heart toward him. God worked in her husband's heart through a recovery program at church, and he overcame his addiction to pornography. The anger and guilt that he projected toward his wife were harder to put aside, but God knew just what was needed to tender this husband's heart. We would consider a bout with breast cancer a bad thing, but when God allowed cancer to grow in this young woman's body and her husband thought he would lose her, he realized how very much he loved her. Because this young wife was willing to take a chance on God's promise to turn what was meant for evil into good, He was able to put her marriage back together His way.

The little boy whose father walked out on his family hurt himself and those who loved him most by making some very poor lifestyle choices. After trying to take control of his pain by harshly controlling the people and circumstances in his life, God intervened and stripped him of most of the things he held dear. In desperation this man turned to God and found the healing and freedom he had been looking for all of his life. God placed people in this man's life to help him rebuild the ruins that his father had left in his heart. Because this husband and father placed his hope in God, his children have witnessed up close God's power to transform the human heart. This man is now a voice of hope to many who are suffering some of the same things he suffered and overcame.

The man with cerebral palsy gave his life to Christ when he was eighteen. He found that God had plans for him that went way beyond playing sports. Once he accepted himself, he found that others accepted him, too. God has brought others with cerebral palsy into his life, and this young man has learned that the most limiting thing in his life was not his physical limitations but the way he let them affect his thinking. Once he had God's perspective on the cerebral palsy, he realized that what God didn't give him in physical strength and coordination He made up for in other gifts and abilities that can be used for the kingdom of God.

The young woman who gave up her dreams as she searched for her significance in all the wrong places came to the end of herself and decided that God's way was, after all, better than hers. She chose to invest her life in raising her precious son and trusting God for all the other things she desired. God gave her opportunities to impact the lives of teenage girls who were on the brink of making the same poor choices that she made. She chose to take the pain of her self-inflicted wounds to God and allow Him to heal her and set her free. She has found her significance in the life she has rebuilt on God's truth.

Down through the ages God has taken what man meant for evil and turned it around for good, but each time it was because the person chose to surrender the pain and circumstances to the power and sovereignty of God.

The most poignant example of God turning what man meant for evil into what He meant for good was when the evil of sinful men nailed His Son to a cross. The plot to kill Jesus was contrived by the very people He came to save. One of His very own betrayed Him for money. Men meant Christ's death for evil, but God meant it as a sacrifice for your sins and mine.

Romans 8:28 says, "And we know that in all things God works for the good of those who love him, who have been called according to his purpose." Do you see the promise? God will bring something good from your wound. But you must first meet the conditions for the promise—that you love Him and are called to His purposes. The good that God wants to bring from the pain of your wound is found in Romans 8:29. God wants you "to be conformed to the likeness of His Son."

God uses the pain in our lives to build Christ-like character in us that is tested and proven true. He uses the pain to teach us to obey His Word and endure with Him in the power of His Spirit. He uses our suffering to grow our faith so that we will hope in Him, believing that though we may not see it yet, God will do everything He promises.

Romans 8:28 does not say that all things are good! They are not. Your wound is not good. Your pain is not good. The sin that wounded you is not good, and any sinful response to your wound or your wounder is not good. But God is able to mysteriously work in all that is not good and bring good from it. Part of the good is the rebuilding of your broken heart so that you can experience the fullness of His glory and His blessing.

Ask God to show you the good He can bring from the pain of your wounded heart.

I would not have learned the truths shared in this book if I had not embraced my painful story and the sovereignty, love, and goodness of God in the midst of it.

I would not have written this book if I had not let God show me the good that He wanted to bring out of my abusive childhood.

If I had not lived through an abusive childhood and experienced God's hope and healing for my wounded heart, I would not be able to offer you His hope and healing as your own.

What my parents meant for evil, God intended for good. God used the pain of my wound to draw me to Himself and to grow my faith in Him. God is using my journey of freedom, healing, and rebuilding to impact the lives of others.

Whatever wounded you may have been meant for evil in your life, but before your heart was broken, God already had a plan in place to turn it around for good. You and I can only see the part of our story that has already been written, but God sees it all. If you will place your wounded heart in His hands, He will redeem your heart and your story.

There is power in your story for you, for others, and for the kingdom of God, so be strong and courageous as you embrace your story.

Embrace your story so that you can connect with the real you.

Embrace your story so that you can see the grace and mercy of God as He redeems it.

Embrace your story so that you can rebuild your heart.

Embrace your story so that God can use it in someone else's life.

Ask God to help you embrace your "I" story so that you can lay it at His feet and watch Him bring good out of what seems so bad.

Reflection & Application

1. Do you find it hard to connect with your own heart and the feelings and emotions that are hidden there? What feelings do you run to when you can't pinpoint what you are truly feeling? It may be anger, fear, shame and guilt, pain and hurt, loneliness, sadness, joy and happiness, emptiness, fulfillment, frustration, discouragement, anxiety, or myriad other feelings.

2. Have you written for yourself a story that is more pleasing to read than your real story? Are you willing to compare your rewritten story with your real story and embrace what is real?

3. If you will embrace your "I" story, how can God use it for your good and the good of others?

Chapter 16

ɶ

Rebuilt for God's Glory

By the time we get to this point most people are torn between the anticipation of what life will look like when they break free from their wounds and the gut feeling that they are chasing a fantasy. I have no idea where your heart is right now, but how I pray that you will place your faith in the healing power of Jesus Christ and courageously hope for the freedom and wholeness that you cannot yet see.

I wish I could tell you that once your heart is rebuilt you will never have to deal with the pain of sin's wounds again. I wish I could assure you that from the time the last brick is laid in the wall of your rebuilt heart not one piece of mortar will ever again be chipped out by sin. How I wish I could promise you that there will be no wrecking ball in your future and that you can live out your life wound-free, but that's not the case. As long as there is sin, there will be wounds; however, you do not have to ever be in bondage to a wound again. You never have to become a prisoner to the pain of a wounded heart.

Jesus Christ did not die to set you free from the bondage of sin so that you could float back and forth between freedom in Him and bondage to your sin or someone else's or to the wounds sin inflicts.

He set you free to stay free! But there's a catch—freedom is your choice. You have to choose to dig in your heels and stand firm in your freedom and healing. You have to choose never to submit to the bondage of sin's wounding power again.

The choice is yours, but you will never make the choice without the Lord Jesus Christ. Jesus heals us and sets us free from the inside out, so to stand in His freedom and healing you must have His Spirit living in you.

Romans 10:9 says, "If you confess with your mouth, 'Jesus is Lord,' and believe in your heart that God raised Him from the dead, you will be saved." Ephesians 2:8-9 tells you that "it is by grace you have been saved through faith—and this not from yourselves, it is the gift of God—not by works, so that no one can boast." If you have received God's salvation, His gift of grace, by faith, then He is your Lord and Savior, and He is asking you to take His hand and let Him lead you on your journey of rebuilding.

If you have never accepted God's gift of salvation by faith, He is offering you the gift of eternal life that Jesus Christ purchased for you when He died on the cross for your sins. All you have to do is tell Him that you want His precious gift and exchange the life you have now for the life He has for you. Once Jesus Christ is your Savior, the Holy Spirit comes to live in your heart to empower you to stand firm in the freedom that Jesus has given you.

Without the power of the Holy Spirit to help you control your responses when the wounding circumstances of life try to steal your joy, your peace, your worth, your confidence, your identity, your significance, and even your physical well-being, you will move right back into the same harmful responses that held you in the prison of your pain before Christ made you whole. If you go back, it won't be long before you will once again be in bondage to a wound.

God never promised us a pain-free life; in fact, he has told us quite the contrary. In John 17 Jesus prayed for His first disciples and for everyone else who would choose to embrace Him as Savior and Lord. One of the things He prayed for you and me is that God the Father would "protect them from the enemy." That is the same enemy that comes only to steal, kill, and destroy, and is looking for someone to devour.

The beginning of 1 Peter 5:8 warns us to "be self-controlled and alert." Verse 9 finishes the instruction telling us to "resist him, standing firm in the faith." Look at that closely. God does not ask you to stand firm in your own strength, but in your faith in Him.

Never forget that your journey of rebuilding and staying rebuilt is a spiritual journey, a journey not of the mind only or the emotions, but of the heart. It is a journey of faith that you will finish only when your heart is surrendered to God and His plans and purposes for your life. Your hope cannot be in your own ability to dull the pain through retribution or denial. *Your hope is in facing the truth about your wound, your pain, and your own inability to respond in a way that brings healing.*

Responding with anger, self-pity, unbelief, or sinful behavior is like putting a bandage on an infected wound so you don't have to look at it. Pretending to be okay or ignoring the pain of your wounded heart only gives it time to fester all the more. You have one hope and that is in placing it all—your wound, your pain, your brokenness, your wounder, your journey—in Jesus' hands and allowing Him to heal your broken heart and redeem what was lost.

Rebuilding the ruins of your broken heart will not be free from doubts and fears. God knows that. He knows every obstacle you will face. He knows every attack Satan will unleash on you. He already knows every time you will stumble, every time you will fall or want to give up, and every time you will struggle with believing that He is working with you and for your good.

Because He knows you will encounter many obstacles in your rebuilding process, God has given you many words of encouragement like these:

Isaiah 41:10, "So do not fear, for I am with you; do not be dismayed, for I am your God. I will strengthen you and help you; I will uphold you with my righteous right hand."

Isaiah 43:1-5, "Fear not, for I have redeemed you; I have summoned you by name; you are mine. When you pass through the waters, I will be with you; and when you pass through the rivers, they will not sweep over you. When you walk through the fire, you will not be burned; the flames will not set you ablaze. For I am the Lord, your God..."

God knows what your journey into freedom, healing, and wholeness will look like and He asks you to trust in Him. Psalm 34:8 is one of my favorite verses because it shows me how gently God woos us to Himself. God invites you and me to "taste and see that the LORD is good."

When I read that verse, a picture comes to mind of feeding a baby and the way a parent barely touches the spoon to the child's lips to give them a taste of what is being offered. The hope is that the child will open wide and take the whole spoonful. That is what God asks of us; just taste His goodness because once we taste it we will want more. Notice that verse doesn't say to taste and see "if" the Lord is good. No, the Lord *is* good!

That is one of His attributes. He just wants you to lay your wound, your pain, your ruins, your past, present, and future in His arms and taste for yourself the magnitude of His goodness.

Once you choose to make this journey with God, how will you stay the course and stay rebuilt? Your best chance of staying on course and out of bondage is to take time every day to read your Bible, God's love letter to you. In God's Word you will see how He wants you to respond when someone hurts you physically, mentally, or emotionally. You will see how He is working on your behalf to equip and empower you for the journey and for standing firm in your freedom. As you meet with God in His Word, He will give you verses that will fill you with the strength and encouragement you need to overcome when you are wounded again with attitudes, behaviors, or words.

No matter what kinds of things tend to hurt your heart, no matter how your pain manifests itself, no matter what your pattern of response to the pain is, the Bible has words that will speak to your heart. That is because the Word of God is living and active. It is adaptable and applicable to each of us as unique individuals. FYI, the Proverbs are a great source of wisdom for dealing with most everything you will encounter.

You know the kinds of offenses that wound your heart, so be on your guard, and stay alert, because the enemy knows what hurts you, too. He will use those offenses to re-wound your heart. Be aware when actions or words are hitting you where it hurts and claim the promises of God's Word that apply to you in that moment. Ask the Holy Spirit to control you so that you can control your response.

Keep the time between being wounded and going to God as short as you possibly can. Write the verses God gives you on cards to carry with you so that they are always at your fingertips. When something happens that hurts you, pull out your cards and read them asking God to help you believe what His Word says about you and about what just happened. Since you and God know the kind of words and actions that are prone to wound you, take them to Him quickly so that you can respond in a way that brings His comfort and healing in your moments of pain.

Remember that God is always waiting for you to cry out to Him, and when you do He hears you and puts all of the resources He has already prepared for you at your disposal. Don't ever hesitate to cry out to God, even when Satan whispers that it won't do any good. Listen to the words of Isaiah 30:18-19, "The Lord longs to be gracious to you; he rises to show you compassion. For the Lord is a God of justice. Blessed are all who wait for him! … How gracious he will be when you cry for help! As soon as he hears, he will answer you."

God will guide you to the people and resources He has handpicked to help you on your journey to freedom and wholeness. Ask Him to show you people who can be trusted with your heart, people who will continually point you to Him.

There is encouragement and accountability when we have a godly person to pull alongside us in our process.

If you diligently go through this process with God and you are still struggling, you may need the help of a good Christian counselor. If you decide to talk with a counselor, please find one who will point you to God and His Word and who knows that he or she is only your helper and that God is your healer.

God has given His children the unique privilege to "approach the throne of grace with confidence, so that we may receive mercy and find grace to help us in our time of need" (Hebrews 4:19). **Take the privilege of going to God in prayer seriously.** Pray for yourself, your journey, your process, and for the one who wounded you. *Nothing will change your heart toward a person or a circumstance faster than taking it to God in prayer.*

God has given you and me godly people, His Word, and the power of His Holy Spirit to become victorious overcomers, but that's not all.

When God created you, He already knew that sin would enter the world, that you would be wounded, and that the time would come when you would be on a journey with Him to rebuild the ruins of your wounded heart. He knew, too, that the enemy would try with all his might to keep you from believing that you can be rebuilt. God in His wisdom designed your brain for the process of rebuilding.

So before you are tempted to believe that freedom, healing, and rebuilding will come to others, but not you; before you believe that no matter how hard you work, the peace and joy of a rebuilt heart will always be just beyond your grasp, let me encourage you to read on.

Doctor Caroline Leaf, a PhD from South Africa, has studied the human brain for over twenty-five years. In her book *Who Switched Off My Brain?* she shares the most incredible findings from her research. I highly recommend that you read this book if you want to know more about how

God equipped your brain to help you rebuild your heart. I cannot do justice to the marvelous scientific facts that she shares, so bear with my layman's insights.

These are the highlights that stood out to me when I read Dr. Leaf's book. As I read her book I was in tears, marveling at what an awesome Creator God we have. We truly do have marvelous bodies that could not possibly be the result of chance. God asks us to do the work of rebuilding, and He gives us everything we need to do what He asks. He took care of every detail, even your brain.

Let me try to summarize what God taught me through Dr. Leaf's book:

As we take in bits of new information through our five senses, memories that we have already built are activated causing us to react to the new information. A burst of chemicals is sent to the part of the brain where memories are stored. Which chemicals are sent depends on the attitudes and emotions that are awakened from our previous memories. Since our brain responds in only one of two ways, either in fear or in faith, it releases either fear chemicals or faith chemicals in response to our emotional state and attitude toward the new information.

Your brain has a small gland that stores emotional perceptions to past experiences and information. These perceptions can be based on either the truth or facts. For example: the fact may be that you don't know how to swim—the truth is you don't know how, but you can learn. As the chemicals that are released go through this gland, they activate our stored emotional perceptions, which tell us either positive or negative things about the information we have taken in. This causes a surge of adrenaline that is either fear based or faith based. This surge is what we call a "gut reaction." We all know that feeling of intense happiness or intense anxiety and fear.

When we take in information it flows back and forth through our brain for 24-48 hours before we make it into a memory. Now this is amazing! There is a structure in the front of our brain that scientists have identified as the structure that gives us "free will." God didn't just leave our choices to chance, because as a piece of information flows to the front of our brain we are able to make a choice through our free will to accept or reject the information. If we reject the information, it literally becomes hot air and leaves the brain. If we choose to think about the information it will become a memory.

If the information is a fear-based memory, the chemicals that attach to it make bulges on the memory structure of the brain that look like thorns. They can actually see this in pictures of the brain! These fear-based memory structures with thorns grow differently than faith-based memories. They spread like weeds in the brain. In pictures of the brain they actually look like a black cloud. Dr. Leaf says that every time we access these fear-based memories it is like taking hold of a thorn bush. It hurts us and the more we think about these memories the stronger and more painful they becomes. This causes us to be stressed, and the chemicals that flow through our bodies as a result make us physically sick.

Before you get discouraged, listen to this. We can make a choice of our will to change the structure of these thorny memories by thinking good, truthful thoughts. This is why God's Word is so important. When we decide that we want to be free and healed from harmful memories we can release those memories through forgiveness, repentance, rejecting anger, and letting go of sinful behaviors.

As we do this, the faith chemicals that are released literally cause the thorns to fall off of the memory structure and a new memory is built over the old memory. But first the thorns have to go. We will still have the old memory, but the pain and negative thoughts associated with it are gone. We can THINK away the thorns of bad or negative memories. This is Romans 12:2 in action, "Be transformed by the renewing of your mind."

I find this next bit of information very interesting, especially since painful memories have such a strong hold on us. It has been proven in the laboratory that all of the faith-based chemicals are stronger than the fear-based chemicals. So why do we hang on to our bad, hurtful memories for so long? Could it be because the enemy keeps them at the forefront of our minds?

But look at this! In just four days we can change the biochemical structure of our brain and begin reversing the negative memories, simply by submitting our free will to God and choosing through the power of the Holy Spirit to believe the truth of God's Word. FOUR DAYS! Researchers have seen the change in the laboratory.

This is what Proverbs 23:7(NASB) means when it says "as he thinks within himself, so is he." God has given us a brain that can think its way either to destruction or to wholeness. The transformation of our lives really does start with a change in the way we think.

Here is another fascinating tidbit from Dr. Leaf's book. There is a small brain in your heart (the organ that pumps our blood, not a spiritual place) that works with your freewill structure to guide your decision making. It is constantly communicating with the brain to act as a checking station, the conscience, to check the accuracy and integrity of your thought life. There is a feedback loop between the heart and the brain that tells us good or bad, accept or reject. When your head and your heart are out of sync, Dr. Leaf says you need to listen to your heart. This is contrary to what we have been taught, isn't it?

But Dr. Leaf poses the question of how many times we know in our hearts that we are about to make a wrong decision, say the wrong thing, or act the wrong way, but we do it anyway?

The heart also secretes a balance hormone that pulls every other system of the body into its rhythm, so when our hearts are in chaos because of choices we are making, so is the rest of the body. When we listen to our hearts, they are at peace and so are we. When we listen to our hearts, God's Word can work His purposes in our lives.

I have only scratched the surface of the amazing things that Dr. Leaf shares in her book. It would be well worth your time for you to read her book for yourself. You will find her contact information in the appendix at the end of this book.

Can you see that God has equipped you in every way to make this journey into freedom, healing, and wholeness? He has given you everything that you need to rebuild the ruins of your wounded heart. All you have to do is choose by faith to partner with Him.

Let me give you my definition of rebuilding the ruins of your broken heart:

Rebuilding the ruins of your wounded heart is the transformation that takes place in your mind, your heart, and your behavior when you choose to let the truth of God replace the painful, destructive thoughts and behaviors that have ruled your life, and in the power of the Holy Spirit you allow God's Word to accomplish its purposes in your heart and life.

God knows that you will never let Him heal your heart and work with Him to rebuild it until you see Him as He truly is. Repentance opens the eyes of your heart to see God.

God knows that until you face the depths of your pain, you will never clearly see the ruins of your brokenness so that you can clear them away and make room for something new and beautiful to be built in their place.

God knows that your heart needs the cleansing grace of grieving to wash away the pain and begin anew with Him.

God knows that coming face to face with your giant, the one who hurt you, will give your heart the empowering courage it needs to move forward with Him into healing and freedom.

And God knows that as you draw on the power of the Holy Spirit to forgive the one who wounded your heart, the chains of your bondage are broken to release you to be rebuilt for His glory.

God has given you His Word to infuse you with truth and life, and He has promised to bring good from all of the bad as you love and obey Him.

Have you have ever watched a structure being built? When my first grandson was younger he and I loved watching construction projects. We watched the building of everything from storage sheds to mega churches.

One thing I learned from each construction site is that when the structure is ready to be raised every builder begins in the same place. Whether he is working with bricks, stones, or boards; whether he is building a house, a shed, a grocery store, or a mega structure; the builder starts on his knees laying the foundation for the structure. That is where we start our rebuilding as well, on our knees in humility before God laying the foundation for our rebuild heart—the foundation of repentance.

From that foundation you will work with God to complete the rebuilding of your heart, His temple. As you work diligently, God will raise you up to stand in awe at the work you have done with Him. Psalm 18:33 (AMP) says that God "makes my feet like hinds' feet [able to stand firmly or make progress on the dangerous heights of testing and trouble]; He sets me securely upon my high places." From your high place with God you will learn to stand in healing and freedom no matter what life brings. From that high place you can *choose* to never again live in the pain of your wounds.

As you rebuild your life with new truth, you will be able to recycle the ruins of your broken heart. You will learn to stop throwing stones from your rubble pile and instead reach into the ruins, clean off some of the stones in your pile of rubble, and use them as remembrance stones of God's faithfulness along your journey to freedom and wholeness.

I remember when I came to that time in my process. I remember placing those stones of remembrance into the wall of my rebuilt heart.

I picked up the stone of rejection and placed it in my wall, for I know that God will never leave me or forsake me (Hebrews 13:5).

I dusted off that stone of condemnation, for there is now, therefore, no condemnation toward me because I am in Christ Jesus (Romans 8:1).

The stone of not being protected went into my wall in a place of prominence, for God is now my shield and protector (Psalm 33:20).

I took the stone of being unloved, polished it, and placed it front and center, for I now have a Father who loves me with an unfailing love (Psalm 90:14).

The stone I cherish most is the stone of my hidden tears. My childhood tears were rejected, but not one of them hit the ground. Psalm 56:8 says God caught them all in a bottle. He held them there, until I rebuilt the ruins of my wounds and was healed; then He gave them back to me as tears of thankfulness, joy, compassion, and love that came, not from a grieving heart, but from a heart made tender by Him.

As your journey into freedom, healing, and wholeness draws to an end, God will call you to a new beginning. Listen to what He says to you in Isaiah 43:18-19:

"Forget the former things; do not dwell on the past.
See, I am doing a new thing!
Now it springs up; do you not perceive it?
I am making a way in the desert and streams in the wasteland."

Can you perceive it? God is doing something new in you! What was once a wasteland of wounds in your heart is becoming a stream of living water, flowing with the life of Christ in you. As you rebuild the ruins of your broken heart, God is taking you to a place where you can hold His hand and walk away from the past, a place where you can live in the reality of Philippians 3:13-14, "Forgetting what is behind and straining toward what is ahead, I press on toward the goal to win the prize for which God has called me heavenward in Christ Jesus."

God wants to do something in your life that you cannot even begin to imagine. First Corinthians 2:9 promises you this, "No eye has seen, no ear has heard, no mind has conceived what God has prepared for those who love him."

God has amazing things in store for you, so stay the course with Him. Don't give up. Let God continue to rebuild you until you are fully rebuilt, because when the ruins of your heart are rebuilt you will know the reality of His promise in Isaiah 61:2-3

> To comfort all who mourn,
>   and provide for those who grieve …
> to bestow on them a crown of
>   beauty instead of ashes,
> the oil of gladness
>   instead of mourning,
> and a garment of praise
>   instead of a spirit of despair.
> They will be called oaks of
>   righteousness,
> a planting of the LORD
> for the display of his splendor.

That is the final outcome of walking out of the bondage of your wounds and into God's freedom, of allowing Him to bind up your broken heart and heal it, and of working with Him to rebuild the ruins of your heart, His temple. You will be "a planting of the Lord for the display of His splendor," and all who see your new, rebuilt life will know that you are indeed an "oak of righteousness."

Reflection & Application

1. If you are choosing the freedom that Christ died to give you, what specific changes will you have to make to ensure that you stay free?

2. How can you "taste and see that the Lord is good"? What are practical, tangible things you can do that will position you to see the goodness of God in your life and painful circumstances?

3. What kinds of actions and words wound your heart? Write down Scripture verses that will comfort you and reassure you when these actions and words are directed your way.

Resources

The following scripture references will be invaluable to you in your healing and rebuilding process, but they are just to get you started.

I was tempted to write out these verses for you so you could reference them quickly. I changed my mind, though, because having to look them up will encourage you to go to God's Word for yourself, read the verses in context, and trust the Holy Spirit to show you even more scriptures He wants you to see. Dig in! There are precious treasures waiting for you.

Anger/Bitterness
Ephesians 4:26-27; Ephesians 4:31-32; James 1:19-20

Anxiety/Worry
Philippians 4:6-7; 1 Peter 5:7

Believing in God's Love for you
Proverbs 8:17; John 15:9; Romans 5:5

Courage
Joshua 1:9; 2 Chronicles 32:7-8

Depression
Deuteronomy 31:8 (AMP); Psalm 40:1-3

Discouragement
Psalm 3:3; John 16:33; 2 Corinthians 4:8

Encouragement
Psalm 31:7; Psalm 62:1-2; Psalm 119:50

Fear
1 John 4:4; Psalm 91:4-5; 2 Timothy 1:7; Isaiah 41:10

Forgiveness
Ephesians 4:32; Colossians 3:13

Guilt and Condemnation
Psalm 51:1-2; Romans 8:1-2

Hope
Romans 15:4; Romans 15:13; Psalm 33:18

Insecurity
Psalm 27:1; Proverbs 18:10; Romans 8:37-39;
2 Corinthians 12:9; Philippians 4:13

Loneliness
1 Samuel 12:22; Psalm 46:1; Matthew 28:20; John 14:18

Peace
Isaiah 54:10; John 14:27; 2 Thessalonians 3:16

Protection
Deuteronomy 33:27; Psalm 9:9; Psalm 91: 9-11

Rejection
John 15:16; Romans 8:31; Ephesians 1:4-6

God's Goodness
Psalm 145:9; Psalm 34:8; Jeremiah 33:11; Nahum 1:7

Trust
Psalm 31:14-15; Psalm 62:8; Psalm 2:12; Proverbs 3:5-6;
Isaiah 30:15

References

Chapter 9
> *Finding My Home: Pathways To Life and The Spirit* by Henri J.M. Nowen, The Crossroad Publishing Company, 2001, pages 101 & 103

Chapter 12
> *The Wounded Heart* by Dr. Dan B. Allender, NAVPRESS, 1990, 105
>
> *The Wounded Heart* by Dr. Dan B. Allender, NAVPRESS, 1990, 202

Chapter 16
> *Who Switched Off My Brain?* by Dr. Caroline Leaf, Switch On Your Brain, 2007

Dr. Leaf's book is available on Amazon.com or by contacting her at www.drleaf.net

Other Books by Edye Burrell

My Garden, God's Classroom:
Spiritual Lessons God Taught a Ditzy Gardener

For more information or to invite Edye to speak, please contact her at
edye@surprisedbygraceministries.com or go to
www.surprisedbygraceministries.com.

LaVergne, TN USA
29 October 2010
202766LV00002B/2/P

Jeremiah 31:3-4
God's promise for you!
Eder